100 Things
to Do Before
You Die

100 Things

to Do Before You Die

Travel Events You Just Can't Miss

Dave Freeman, Neil Teplica,
and the Editors of
WhatsGoingOn.com

With Jennifer Coonce

Taylor Publishing Company
Dallas, Texas

Designed by Hespenheide Design
Cover photos: **Paro Tsechu**—Marie Brown; **Icarus Cup Masquerade Flights (Coupe Icare)**—26th Icarus Cup; **Naadam**—Pat Lanza/Boojum Expeditions; **Wanaka RipCurl World Heli-Challenge**—Tony Harrington at The Photo Shop, Wanaka

Published by Taylor Publishing Company
1550 West Mockingbird Lane
Dallas, Texas 75235
www.taylorpub.com

Library of Congress Cataloging-in-Publication Data:
Freeman, Dave.
    100 things to do before you die : travel events you just can't miss / by Dave Freeman, Neil Teplica and the editors of WhatsGoingOn.com ; co-written by Jennifer Coonce.
        p.   cm.
    ISBN 0-87833-243-X
    1. Special events Guidebooks.   2. Festivals Guidebooks.   I. Teplica, Neil.   II. Coonce, Jennifer.
III. Title.   IV. Title: One hundred things to do before
you die.
GT3405.F73   1999
394.2—dc21   99-37504
                                                                                          CIP

10 9 8 7 6 5 4 3 1

Printed in the United States of America

"In leaving home one learns life.
You travel. Travelling is victory!
You shall return with much wisdom."

Joseph Conrad
An Outcast of the Islands
1896

Contents

The Icons

 Can See It on TV

 Celebrity Potential

 Civic Pride

 Dangerous

 Down & Dirty

 Ear Candy

 Family Affair

 Gay and Lesbian Interest

 Gluttony

 Grandma Approved

 Gross Things

 Jock Appeal

 Loud As Hell

 Mother Nature

 One of a Kind

 Out of the Way

 Potential to See Blood

 Reenactments

 Religious Fervor

 Shoppertunity

 Snob Appeal

Introduction

This life is a short journey. How can you make sure you fill it with the most fun and that you visit all the coolest places on earth before you pack those bags for the very last time?

Rituals, festivals, and other events are the essence of life and the most intense concentration of cultural experience one can find. They give understanding to travel destinations, serving as a window into what the rest of the world believes in, treasures, celebrates, and holds true. Sometimes they even offer a glimpse into the past or the future. Furthermore, these celebrations are often the most emotional and rewarding experiences of traveling. They're awaiting your participation. So what are you waiting for? Start packing!

Paris is a beautiful city and a pleasure to visit any day of the year. But you have never felt Gallic pride in full effect until you've danced with a French firefighter there on Bastille Day. Every minute in India seems saturated with mysterious Hindu beliefs and symbolism. But when this religious fervor comes together in the "juggernaut" at Puri's Rath Yatra, you really start to understand what Hinduism is all about. And there is no better way to find out more about America's spirit of ingenuity and competitiveness than by experiencing the wacky and outrageous World Championship Punkin' Chunkin' in Delaware.

In this book, we've selected what we believe to be the world's one hundred most stimulating and inspiring events. We've scoured the globe, traveled millions of miles, and talked to the people who have made the pilgrimage, danced in the streets, run with the bulls, and sampled the local vibe. This list should serve as a jumping-off point for determining what's worth checking out and then checking off your list.

Some of these events are large and some are small. Some require lots of preparation and some are easy to participate in. Some are very expensive and difficult to attend and others are open to everyone. But they all have something special that really sets them apart. Whether well known or obscure, they all demand your attention. Like a good meal, the list offers a wide range of tastes and flavors, from elated to somber, from ancient to modern, from reserved to raucous, and from significant to just plain silly. There is something here for every mood and mindset. There's probably something right in your own backyard.

While the intent of this book is primarily to fuel your dreams, we also wanted to provide up-to-the-minute resources for planning your adventures. For the latter, we have created a unique tool. With each event in this book you will find a corresponding "web coordinate" URL. When you visit this page on the WhatsGoingOn.com website, you will find upcoming event dates, contact telephone numbers, and web addresses to help you plan and turn your dreams into reality. Information and contacts for many of these events are always changing, so you have, in effect, purchased a book that will never become out of date.

So what are you waiting for? Get off your butt and create a fabulous memory or two before you exit this life. And be sure to let us know how your adventure turns out. Bon voyage!

Dave Freeman and Neil Teplica

Disclaimer

Be physically and mentally prepared when you participate in many of the events described in this book. Be warned that aside from having fun, you could be crushed, gored, burned, frozen, drowned, run over, electrocuted, infected, punctured, or dehydrated. You could get hit with a mallet, arrow, or pumpkin. In short, you run the risk of serious or possibly fatal infury. So be careful. And don't say we didn't warn you.

The USA and Canada

Iditarod Dog Sled Race

World Extreme Skiing Championships

Calgary Stampede and Exhibition

Testicle Festival

Custer's Last Stand Reenactment

Burning Man Project

National Finals Rodeo

Academy Awards Ceremony

Pageant of the Masters

Navajo Nation Fair

Roswell UFO Encounter

World Cow Chip Throwing Contest

Mangum Rattlesnake Derby

Spamarama

Art Car Weekend

New Orleans Jazz and Heritage Festival

Mardi Gras

Greenwich Village Halloween Parade

New Year's Eve in Times Square

World Championship Punkin' Chunkin'

Battle of Gettysburg Reenactment

National Hollerin' Contest

Locations vary for Coaster Con and
North American Rainbow Gathering

Iditarod Sled Dog Race

Anchorage to Nome, Alaska, USA

GPS Lat: 64.50922 N Lon: 165.41519 W

Every year, human adventurers and canines join together to confront the coldest weather and the toughest terrain. The legendary Iditarod Sled Dog Race has set the standard for sled dog racing worldwide. Known as "The Last Great Race on Earth," the competition begins on the first Saturday in March in Anchorage and covers 1,150 miles to Nome.

Annual, March
(first Saturday)

A musher begins the race with sixteen dogs—a team that stretches 80 feet from the leader's nose to the musher at the back of the sled. That's about as long as an eighteen-wheel truck (only a lot cuter). As soon as the musher calls out, "Hike, okay!" the dogs take off. Contrary to Hollywood lore, no one yells "Mush!" In fact, the pack is driven by the musher's voice alone, not by reins. This type of dog-human relationship is extremely affectionate and sometimes takes on an ESP quality.

Once the race gets underway, there are long stretches of time in which the team runs on autopilot (good trails and fair weather conditions permitting). The musher is free to pop a favorite musher-mix tape into a Walkman and enjoy the scenery.

Trail breakers usually ride ahead of lead teams and clear the area. There are more than twenty checkpoints at which the musher must stop. These are the only times that he or she can receive any outside assistance, get food and shelter, attend to the dogs, and handle any other business without breaking race rules.

The year 1973 marked the first Iditarod. Many believed it was crazy to head out into the vast Alaskan wilderness. However, those who didn't packed up their arctic parkas, snowshoes, and 2,000 dog booties per team (dogs need protection from the cold, too!) and took part in what was to become Alaska's best-known sporting event.

Since then, thousands of people have been infected with musher-mania. Volunteers and fans come out in droves to be part of the Last Great Race on Earth.

As the nose of the first dog crosses the finish line, the celebrations begin. A huge crowd lines the "chute" down Nome's Front Street as the city's fire siren blares. After about seventeen days of lining the chute, folks get tired. However, each musher is entitled to a big welcome. Even the last team back gets special recognition—the Red Lantern Award, for those so far back they need a light to find their way home.

When You Go:

If you'd rather not brave the cold on Front Street, then check out the celebration at the Nome Convention Center.

> "the standard for sled dog racing worldwide"

Over 2,000 people come out to see the mushers pick up their victory belt buckle and finisher patches. Every musher gets a chance to speak, and the awards are given out. Those who aren't back in time for the main banquet are honored at the Red Lantern Banquet. Better late than never, right?

Web Coordinate:

www.whatsgoingon.com/100things/iditarod

Iditarod Trail Comm, Inc./Jim Brown

World Extreme Skiing Championships

Chugach Mountain Range, Valdez, Alaska, USA

GPS Lat: 61.08336 N Lon: 146.30237 W

Annual, March/April

Each spring, thirty-eight of the world's craziest and best skiers compete in the World Extreme Skiing Championships (WESC) on the slopes of the Chugach Mountain range, which encircles the Alaskan port of Valdez. The competition's slopes are at a 35- to 55-degree angle, with descents of 2,000 to 3,000 feet. One fall and a skier, traveling 65 miles per hour, can die instantly. This is the most insane skiing competition in the world. WESC president Mark Johnson has said of the championship skiers, "These competitors are some of the best athletes in the world. The ability these athletes have to draw their line right along the edge, while being very aware of what lies on the other side, is impressive." What that means is that they come close to death without actually dying, usually.

This competition is the culmination of over a half-dozen very tough qualifying events around the world, including competitions in Japan, South America, Europe, and the USA. At the World Extreme Skiing Championships, there are three days of competitive skiing, with the terrain and slopes getting progressively more difficult. Rocks, narrow gorges, and sheer cliffs are part of the mix. Skiers are judged on several standards, including aggressiveness, fluidity, control, and technical ability. As the event progresses, competitors accumulate scores from each day. For the finals, the top fifteen men and top four women are chosen.

Because of the danger of this event, the WESC takes pains to make things as safe as possible. The proceedings are begun with a safety meeting, evacuation helicopters are on hand to help fallen skiers, and snow machines refresh the course so skiers don't end up skiing on ice. The preliminary elimination round increases safety, as

Tony Stone Images/Joe McBride

only skiers who can actually win the elimination round make the final run; losers in the elimination round can't ski in the finals, so they aren't further exposed to injury. Says Johnson, "We want people to come here and have fun. To walk away saying, 'This place rips!'"

Over a thousand spectators and competitors visit the snowy Chugach Mountains near Valdez each year to watch the World Extreme Skiing Championships and pump up their adrenaline. Black Diamond ski jockeys leave quite humbled! If you want to compete next year, either do superbly in the qualifiers, or apply by sending in your "ski portfolio" and a demonstration video. Then sit back and wait for the phone to ring.

When You Go:

Valdez is 115 miles east of Anchorage. You can fly, but the drive is worth it. If you take Richardson Highway, you'll be inundated with beautiful scenery—alpine meadows, waterfalls, glaciers, and mountains. Take binoculars and a small radio to the competition. The P.A. announcements are simulcast on a short-range FM stereo transmitter to help you follow the action. Be aware that the competition site is 40 miles from the nearest phone.

Web Coordinate:

www.whatsgoingon.com/100things/extreme

"the most insane skiing competition in the world"

Navajo Nation Fair

Window Rock, Arizona, USA

GPS Lat: 35.66666 N Lon: 109.05000 W

Annual, September
(one week)

Welcome to Dinetah! This unique and beautiful corner of the Southwest is the homeland of the Navajo (or Diné) people. It sprawls out across Arizona and parts of New Mexico and Utah and functions as a semi-autonomous, self-governing region with over 150,000 inhabitants from America's largest Native American tribe.

Every September, the Navajo Nation Fair unites Navajos from all over for the world's largest Native American gathering. It is a great opportunity to experience the ancient traditions and modern realities of Navajo life on the reservation.

Navajos definitely have their own way of doing things. The fair blends all the typical elements of more standard county fairs with the Navajos' highly complex set of beliefs and rites. After checking out the livestock show or whirling around on some carnival rides, you can watch Gourd Dancing, the Drum-Off Competition, or the Grand Pow Wow.

One of the biggest events during the week is the Free Barbecue Feed, where over 10,000 Navajos chow down on more than 2,800 pounds of beef that's specially cooked in big pits covered with thin sheets of steel and piles of dirt. The Feed began as a way for local businesses to say thank you to the Navajos for their patronage and has turned into the biggest reunion of friends, families, and neighbors from all over the reservation.

Another highlight at the fair is a unique twist on the typical beauty contest, the Navajo Nation Pow Wow Princess Pageant. There's no swimsuit competition here; contestants are judged on their dancing ability, "traditional talent," and contributions to the community. The lucky winner represents the Nation at Native American events all over the country.

You'll also want to stick around for the Navajo Nation Indian Professional Rodeo. Navajos have a reputation as expert horse handlers and herders, and this "Native American only" show highlights their gutsy rodeo style. Events include steer wrestling, calf roping, breakaway roping, and barrel racing.

> "experience the ancient traditions and modern realities of Navajo life"

Take some cash, as there will be plenty of crafts for sale. Look out for intricately designed Navajo rugs and blankets featuring bold geometric patterns. You should also find plenty of silver and turquoise jewelry (another Navajo specialty). Save a few bucks to treat yourself to a traditional Navajo meal of stewed mutton and fry bread. It's so good we're sure you'll say a big "ahéheé" (that means "thank you" in Navajo).

When You Go:

Because of their religious beliefs, most Navajos prefer not to have pictures taken. Always ask permission first. While in Window Rock, plan to drop by the Navajo Nation Museum. You'll have the chance to learn all about Navajo history, religion, and arts and crafts. While driving around Navajo Country, keep your radio tuned to KTNN AM 660. This station, known as "the Voice of the Navajo Nation," is run by Navajos and offers music and local news in both English and Navajo.

Web Coordinate:

www.whatsgoingon.com/100things/navajo

Navajo Nation Museum

Academy Awards Ceremony

Los Angeles, California, USA

GPS Lat: 34.36666 N Lon: 118.20000 W

The most desirable 13.5 inches in the movie world don't belong to any adult movie star; they belong to the Oscar statuette. Every March, celebrities and film fans gather live or in front of televisions to watch cinema's most scintillating and exclusive night.

Annual, late March

(Sunday evening)

Since 1929, the Academy of Motion Picture Arts and Sciences has been honoring the achievements of those who make movies happen. What began as a banquet affair in a hotel has turned into a multimedia auditorium and television production with millions of viewers worldwide. You can be sure that the low, low 1929 price of $10 won't get you into the Oscars anytime soon. Heck, being a member of the Academy doesn't even guarantee you a ticket. Only 300 seats are reserved for over 6,000 members. That means that even the bigwigs have to rely on the dumb luck of a lottery.

Those Academy members who use their powers to assist them in getting non-sanctioned guests tickets are subject to excommunication from the Academy. Remarkably, two or three such expulsions happen every year. So the question remains—how does a desperate fan cajole her or his way into an event filled with more stars than the Milky Way? If you scoff at the notion of joining the bathroom attendants' union, perhaps you could be one of those seat-fillers or ushers you've heard so much about. Unfortunately, you'll need a connection to get one of these plum jobs, too. The best investment you can make is putting in a few years of cozying up to a studio head or a performer.

A final (and perfectly legal) way you can score a couple of seats is by placing an ad on the Academy Awards telecast. Sponsors are usually awarded two tickets for each thirty seconds of advertising they run. Thirty-second spots on the Academy Awards have gone for about $1 million in recent years, though, so this may not be the most economical way to sit within spitting distance of John Travolta.

Whether you're inside the auditorium or outside watching the stars arrive, simply enjoy the drama as it unfolds. The night is sure to be filled with memorable moments. No matter who gets the Oscar (probably not you), there will be plenty to discuss at the parties afterwards. Roll up your sleeves; the party's just begun!

Russell Einhorn/STAR MAX, Inc.

When You Go:

Wake up very early. Make sure your hair and makeup people arrive in plenty of time to adequately primp you. Give yourself ample time to get there—that pre-Oscar traffic can be dreadful! Finding a personal assistant is vital. You'll need someone to take care of the little things—like helping you out of the limo and making sure toilet paper isn't stuck to your shoes. Finally, take some raw meat to throw—it will keep the Oscar hounds at bay.

Web Coordinate:

www.whatsgoingon.com/100things/academy

"cinema's most scintillating and exclusive night"

Pageant of the Masters

Laguna Beach, California, USA

GPS Lat: 33.53990 N Lon: 117.76072 W

The Pageant of the Masters is the ultimate expression of life imitating art. For
over sixty-five years, this two-month celebration of art and commerce has been
the raison d'être for the seaside resort of
Laguna Beach.

Annual, July/August

The event began during the depths
of the Great Depression, when the citi-
zenry of this Pacific Coast town sought a means of bolstering the local
economy. Laguna Beach, long an enclave of artists and craftspeople,
inaugurated its first Festival of the Arts in 1932. The organizers incorporated a bit of entrepreneurial flair, adding spectacle into the mix.
The locals outfitted themselves as subjects of artwork and stood in
front of painted backdrops in imitation of master paintings.

The pageant has come a long way from those humble beginnings.
These days, you can view *tableaux vivants*, or "living pictures,"
which are painfully exact recreations of famous masterpieces, with
living models. The performers, in suspended animation, appear to be
part of the painting as the entire work is wheeled onto the stage. A
full orchestra and vocal music accompanies each tableau, and a com-
mentator introduces each work. The two-hour show takes place
every evening in a gorgeous canyon amphitheater.

The program changes every summer and includes a varied selection of about thirty-five works grouped around a broad theme. In the
same evening you might view works like Winslow Homer's *Breezing
Up*, Michelangelo's *Pieta*, and the Korean War Memorial in Washing-
ton D.C. The works are ordered according to narrative value, culminating in the traditional conclusion to each year's show: a startling
recreation of Da Vinci's masterwork, *The Last Supper*.

Artisans of the Pharaoh died for their handiwork. Monet suffered
cataracts, Van Gogh suffered psychoses, and Warhol suffered that wig

of his. Just imagine the suffering of physically imitating fixed art. Over 140 cast members from the community, ages eight through eighty, are painted and placed just as the Masters would have them, holding anatomically inconceivable poses for a full two minutes. The result is amazingly true to form. Rumor has it that a pigeon once flew down and perched on one of the living statues.

Many of the performers have been a part of the show for years, and the audience misses out on the practical jokes played by these veterans. It is not unusual for the apostles of *The Last Supper* to be wearing hula skirts under the table!

When You Go:

The Pageant of the Masters is actually the focal point of the Laguna Beach Festival of the Arts, which features a juried show of over 160 area artists. The festival is open during the day and also features art workshops, demonstrations, and live entertainment. In case you're broke or cheap, local residents say you

> "the ultimate expression of life imitating art"

can climb up the steep hill behind the amphitheater for a great but mildly obstructed view of the pageant. Don't forget your binoculars.

Web Coordinate:

www.whatsgoingon.com/100things/masters

World Championship Punkin' Chunkin'

Lewes, Delaware, USA

GPS Lat: 38.78028 N Lon: 075.14978 W

Annual, November
(first weekend)

World Championship Punkin' Chunkin' embodies the true spirit of American ingenuity and competitiveness—given a challenge (even an inane one), no true American backs down. In Lewes, Delaware, things get unruly when competitors blast, launch, and propel pumpkins for the sole purpose of winning. Convoluted techniques and high-powered machinery are what Punkin' Chunkin' is all about, ever since it was conceived by a couple of testosteronally enhanced dreamers in the mid-1980s.

Viewing the 73-foot pneumatic cannons, centrifugal chunkers, and spring-loaded catapults, you might assume that Punkin' Chunkin' had gone terribly, terribly awry. But no. Monster machines were part of the original diabolical plans of Bill Thompson and Trey Melson in 1986 when they challenged John Ellsworth to a duel to see who could build a machine to chuck a pumpkin the farthest. The pumpkineers turned out to Thompson's farm with machines composed of assorted ropes, tubes, pulleys, garage door springs, poles, and car frames. The top throw was 128 feet and 2 inches, a record that has been shattered to pieces many, many times since the history-making first chunk. These days, chunkers aspire to beat records of over three-quarters of a mile!

Over two dozen teams show off their pumpkin-hurling master-pieces to tens of thousands of spectators on Punkin' Chunkin' week-end. Enter a diesel-powered, spring-loaded, centrifugally oriented, or otherwise insane invention and call it something like "The Nullifier," "The Invalidator," or "The Besmircher," and you'll fit right in. Pumpkins must weigh 8 to 10 pounds and they must leave the machine intact. No explosive fuel is permitted. Divisions include Youth,

Bob Savage and Aquarian Images Photographic Services

Human Powered (manually locked and loaded), Unlimited (motorized), Centrifugal (like windmills with attitude), and Pneumatic (cannons powered by compressed air or bottled gas). The machines that chunk the pumpkins thousands of feet certainly don't lack signs of imagination. At these World Championships, you can find a mishmash of machines, including medieval catapults, machines powered by bicycles, surgical tubing stretched across two telephone poles, and huge wooden towers with ropes and pulleys that are "cocked" by a harnessed team member running out into the field. But that's what's so fun about World Championship Punkin' Chunkin'. You never know what they'll think of next!

When You Go:

Needless to say, don't wear your Sunday best to Punkin' Chunkin'. Since heavy rainfall is a serious possibility at this time of year, you'll want plenty of rain gear—we're talking boots, tarps, and floppy hats. If you can bear living and breathing punkin' chunkin', camping at the official Punkin' Chunkers campground is usually available. It's not a bad idea, since hearing chunker stories is half the fun of attending.

"the true spirit of American ingenuity and competitiveness"

Web coordinate:

www.whatsgoingon.com/100things/punkinchunkin

Coaster Con

Location Varies, USA

GPS Varies

Have you ever wanted to whirl till you hurl? You can get your chance at the American Coaster Enthusiasts' (ACE) Coaster Con. This is a nauseating yet exhilarating thrill-fest, and it has roamed the country every summer for over twenty years in search of the wildest roller coasters America has to offer.

Annual, June

If you can stomach the continual loops and dips of steel beasts and rickety vintage wooden coasters, join some of the 5,000 certified ACE members for the ride of your life. This hardcore group lives for the bliss of being strapped willingly into a flying asylum.

Coaster Con is a road trip of sorts, usually hitting several amusement parks over several days. Favorites over the years have included Kennywood Park near Pittsburgh, Santa Cruz Beach Boardwalk in California, and the home of the first Coaster Con, Busch Gardens in Williamsburg, Virginia.

During Coaster Con, banquets, exhibits, and parties offer plenty of time to get to know other coaster crazies. But most ACErs can't wait until the divine moment when the park shuts down to the public and they get ERT (Exclusive Ride Time) on the most menacing roller coasters, which they ride over and over and over again. Sometimes ERT is offered first thing in the morning, maybe the best time to shake up your ol' digestive tract.

The record number of consecutive rides ever managed by a deranged Coaster Con daredevil was on "Rebel Yell" at Kings Dominion in Doswell, Virginia. Some crazy guy went 102 times around the four-row beauty, which climbs up 44 feet in the air and features a loop, a sidewinder, a double corkscrew, and breakneck velocity in total darkness.

What would possess someone to inflict himself with what seems like sheer torture? The only torture for ACErs at Coaster Con seems to be waiting for the front or back seat in the coaster train—purists prefer the extremes that the front or back seats of a coaster can provide.

The first Coaster Con was launched in 1978, in celebration of the movie aptly entitled *Roller Coaster*, starring Henry Fonda, George Segal, and Susan Strasberg. The film fea-
tured a *Speed*-ish psycho who plants a bomb on a roller coaster that will explode if the coaster slows down. The unlucky passengers of the coaster are forced to endure a five-hour marathon until the mad bomber is apprehended. Pass the Alka Seltzer!

> "a nauseating yet exhilarating thrill-fest"

When You Go:

The folks at ACE will help you with everything—hotels, transportation, park admission, and even picnic lunches for your trembling tummy. Keep in mind that they have other events all over the country all year round. The organizers recommend getting plenty of sleep before Coaster Con starts, as the ERTs usually take place very early in the morning or after the park closes at night. They also suggest you take along plenty of sunscreen.

Web Coordinate:

www.whatsgoingon.com/100things/coaster

Steel Phantom photo courtesy of Kennywood Entertainment

North American Rainbow Gathering

Location Varies, USA

GPS Varies

The Rainbow Family is living proof that American hippie culture did survive the 1970s. For two weeks each year, around 20,000 members of the Family converge on a campground in the USA for the biggest celebration of holistic living in the world at the North American Rainbow Gathering. "It's a healing festival,"

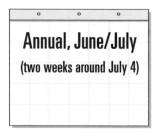

Annual, June/July

(two weeks around July 4)

explains Rainbow Brother Rob Savoye. "We are healing ourselves and healing the Earth. We show people alternative lifestyles. . . . We can have a gathering the size of a city, and it works." It's been working since 1972, when the gathering first happened.

The highlight comes on July 4, when everyone at the Rainbow Gathering comes together to pray for peace and for healing the Earth. "After sunrise, people come to the meadow," says Savoye. "They sit around and pray for peace. Around noon, people gather into a circle or spiral, holding hands. Sometimes it's up to a mile across, and you can barely see the other side of the circle. Then everybody chants 'Om' together. It shakes the mountainside, you know."

During the prayer, a parade of children enters the circle with banners and instruments, dressed in their "festival finest." Then the huge group resumes chanting, lifting their arms into the air and cheering. The rest of the day is a big party with lots of food. "Everyone puts on their best hippie backwoods clothing," says Savoye.

Organizing a community of 20,000 people to live peaceably together for two weeks is no small feat. Still, no one is in charge of the gathering; the gathering relies on people to volunteer to do what needs to be done. Even without a leader, the campground is organized. People separate themselves into distinct camps. Depending on your preference, for example, you can visit the Gay Camp, the camp

> "the biggest
> celebration of
> holistic living in
> the world"

for Hare Krishnas, or the Barbarian Camp for teenagers. Or join the Kiddie Village, where most families pitch their tents and teepees. This camp is fastidiously kept up, with plenty of good food and high hygienic standards. Monitors watch the children as they frolic in an open meadow reserved for them.

When most of the Rainbow Gathering clears out, a few hundred people stay around to clean up the area. Then they leave the seemingly utopian society. Says Savoye, "We all go back home to Babylon after we leave."

When You Go:

The location of the gathering isn't chosen until a few weeks before. Check out the WhatsGoingOn.com website to keep up with what's new and where the Gathering is each year. Be a good Samaritan and volunteer to help out before, after, or during the gathering. Be aware that marijuana is a casual part of the North American Rainbow Gathering, except in the Kiddie Village.

Web coordinate:

www.whatsgoingon.com/100things/rainbow

Photo by Rob Savoye

Mardi Gras

New Orleans, Louisiana, USA

GPS Lat: 30.06584 N Lon: 089.93135 W

In the Big Easy, *"Laissez les bon temps rouler"* means "Let the good times roll!"

Since 1699, New Orleans has hosted the most reckless nonstop party in the USA. The Mardi Gras season officially begins on Epiphany (January 6), but the festivities reach a crescendo on Shrove Tuesday, the day before Lent begins.

Annual, January/ February

(week prior to Shrove Tuesday)

Hence the name Mardi Gras, or "Fat Tuesday."

Mardi Gras is actually a complex collection of many celebrations, some public and some private. Planning of the festivities is done chiefly by local social organizations, called krewes. They often take their names from mythology, like Endymion, Bacchus, or Orpheus. Many krewes are well over a century old and have their own traditions and eccentricities. Krewes are an almost exclusively male-dominated bastion, with the exception of the all-female Krewe of Venus. For the record, diet-guru Richard Simmons is a card-carrying member of Bacchus, and local son Harry Connick Jr. founded the Krewe of Orpheus in 1994.

The backbone of the spectacle is the infamous bunch of parades that the krewes stage in the few weeks before Mardi Gras. Each parade typically takes a theme, usually borrowed from mythology, history, or Hollywood, and each always includes a court of mock royalty.

As the floats and marchers wind through the French Quarter and Garden District, krewe members throw plastic beads and aluminum "doubloons" at the screaming crowds. The most coveted keepsakes, hand-painted coconuts, are passed out during the Zulu Aid and Social Club parade. The coconuts used to be thrown at the crowds, but this practice had to be stopped due to insurance liability. The seventy or so parades snarl traffic for hours and cost the city millions of dollars, but no one seems to mind.

Louisiana Office of Tourism

The krewes also stage over 150 private, invitation-only balls during the Mardi Gras season. The hottest ticket is the Krewe of Rex/Krewe of Comus ball, which takes place at the New Orleans Municipal Auditorium on Fat Tuesday. The round ballroom is separated down the middle by a huge divider, and each krewe holds its own separate party. Then at midnight the divider recedes and the parties spill together as the Queen of Comus is presented to the King of Rex. Don't worry if you aren't invited, because this Meeting of the Courts is televised locally. And there are still another million ways to entertain yourself at Mardi Gras.

When You Go:

Hotel rooms are usually booked eight months in advance for Mardi Gras week. Bring comfortable shoes, because you will be doing plenty of walking. If you plan on wearing a costume (and you should), create something with layers that can be easily removed or added— the temperature can fluctuate considerably from afternoon to evening. And remember, the New Orleans cult classic song "There Ain't Nowhere to Pee on Mardi Gras Day" was inspired by a carnival goer.

> "the most reckless nonstop party in the USA"

Web Coordinate:

www.whatsgoingon.com/100things/mardigras

New Orleans Jazz and Heritage Festival

New Orleans, Louisiana, USA

GPS Lat: 29.95000 N Lon: 090.06666 W

It's always funky time in New Orleans— but the New Orleans Jazz and Heritage Festival is the funkiest. Every year, New Orleans hosts the hippest and most varied display of a truly American art form, which is often called the greatest music

> **Annual, last weekend in April through first weekend in May**

festival in the world. You can't resist a weekend of indulgence, complete with music from zydeco to bluegrass and food such as pheasant, quail, and andouille gumbo and alligator po-boys.

In 1969, Mahalia Jackson, Duke Ellington, Pete Fountain, Al Hirt, and (yes) Woody Allen jammed on the first Jazz Festival's stage, joining 300 of their fellow musicians to entertain a crowd of about half that number. Today, nearly half a million people travel to New Orleans each year for one of the world's most important musical and cultural events. Musicians like Jimmy Buffet, Fats Domino, Ray Charles, Herbie Hancock, Willie Nelson, and James Taylor play the stages of the prestigious festival.

The New Orleans sensory overload of heritage, music, food, crafts, and culture is channeled into a ten-day cultural melting pot. More than a dozen stages host over 4,000 musicians, with offerings of rhythm and blues, gospel, zydeco, ragtime, Cajun, African-Caribbean, folk, Latin, rock, rap, country, and bluegrass, to name a few.

In the evening, in addition to the scheduled big-name shows at the festival, New Orleans's bars and clubs offer a large assortment of live music not officially associated with the Jazz-Fest. Every bowling alley and record store is hopping all night, every night during the festival. Those serious about live music can steer clear of the commercialized corporate restaurant chains and find real gems at some of the more divey joints.

When all the culture and music leaves you hungry for a little more than mind-food, you can try over one hundred varieties of Louisiana cuisine, a gastrointestinal orgy of everything from alligator pie to *cochon de lait*. The fabulous food served up at the New Orleans Jazz Fest is almost as famous as the music.

> "the hippest and most varied display of a truly American art form"

Everything you ever wanted to know about crafts (if you ever wanted to know anything) is spread throughout the grounds of the Jazz Festival. From Mardi Gras Indian costumes to handmade instruments, there's plenty to buy. Then there's the heritage tent, where you can spend days and days learning about music, art, and food—that is, if you can stand any more stimulation.

When You Go:

Airline tickets and hotel rooms go quickly to the New Orleans Jazz Fest's thousands of international and domestic visitors. If your budget restricts, you can fly into Baton Rouge and drive an hour to New Orleans. Maybe you can stay on the couch of a friend of a cousin of a friend. Stop by one of the famous drive-through margarita stands, but then drive to the corner and get out of your car—no drinking and driving! When you're done grooving, don't miss the outrageousness of the French Quarter.

Web coordinate:

www.whatsgoingon.com/100things/jazzfest

Louisiana Office of Tourism

31

Custer's Last Stand Reenactment (Little Big Horn Days)

Hardin, Montana, USA

GPS Lat: 45.73189 N Lon: 107.61336 W

Annual, June
(weekend closest to June 25)

Mere mention of the state of Montana conjures images of America's legendary wide-open spaces. Home of the Unabomber, haven to militias, and the "Land of the Big Sky," Montana embodies all that is the fighting independent spirit of the USA. Here every summer, in a little town called Hardin, a four-day festival offers a historical reenactment of one of America's bloodiest moments, the Battle of Little Big Horn, also known as Custer's Last Stand.

A cast of nearly 300 reenacts Custer's Last Stand 6 miles west of Hardin, on Highway 87. The event site is near where the actual battle took place on June 25, 1876.

The participants, decked out in full regalia, gallop about in a tortuously choreographed game of Cowboys and Indians, but the gun and arrow play does not match the magnitude and gore of the real battle. According to some sources, the original battle featured 210 soldiers from the Seventh Cavalry getting pummeled, scalped, and mutilated by 7,000 tribespeople from the Lakota, Crow, Cheyenne, and Arapaho Nations. Certainly one of the most controversial and mysterious conflicts fought on American soil, the hour-long battle (which, according to Chief Two Moons, "took about as long as it takes for a hungry man to eat his dinner") has been the source of endless dialogue among historians.

Some reenactors in Custer's Last Stand come from far away to be a part of the furious battle (for example, one gentleman regularly flies in from New Zealand to participate). However, most of the cast is from the Hardin area, and many are descendants of early area homesteaders or of Indian scouts who rode with Custer. Chief Sitting Bull and General Custer are portrayed by actors who bear a close physical resemblance to their subjects. Narration for the battle is provided by Chief Sitting Bull. His remarks are based on the translations of Chief Medicine Crow.

Over the years, the reenactment has been filmed by news teams from all over the world, been the subject of numerous documentaries, and been used for the motion picture *Legend of Crazy Horse*.

More than 15,000 viewers show up to watch the bloody performance, which is repeated several times throughout the weekend. Though Custer is never going to win, it's definitely thrilling to watch this twisted piece of history come to life.

> "a historical reenactment of one of America's bloodiest moments"

When You Go:

The battle reenactment is the focal point of Hardin's Little Big Horn Days. Highlights include the 1876 Military Ball (a reenactment hosted by General Custer and his wife Libby) and the Little Big Horn Symposium. Other events include a crafts show, a book fair, quilt shows, chuckwagon barbecues, and a parade. For those hoping to film Custer's Last Stand for their home video archives, take note: you can't. Video cameras are strictly prohibited at the battle reenactment.

Web Coordinate:

www.whatsgoingon.com/100things/custer

Custer's Last Stand

Testicle Festival

Rock Creek Lodge, Clinton, Montana, USA

GPS Lat: 46.66667 N Lon: 113.70000 W

At the Rock Creek Lodge in Clinton, Montana, grannies mingle with biker dudes, college girls flirt with ranch hands, and city folk toast the townies. What is the cause for this show of unity and unbridled fun? Yes, it's time again for the notoriously riotous Testicle Festival, the bawdiest and most absurd festival in the USA.

Annual, September

Every year, over 4,500 pounds of those mysterious, life-giving rocks that once dangled between the legs of some rather unfortunate bulls are fried up and served as "Rocky Mountain Oysters," or "Cowboy Caviar." Castrating male cattle has been going on since ranching started. "You don't waste any part of the animal. It's the cowboy ethic and also the Indian ethic," explains Rod "The Baron of Balls" Lincoln, proprietor of the Rock Creek Lodge. Rod has his nuts inspected by the USDA because "Everybody is sue-happy these days."

The Testicle Festival offers a lot more than just an "oyster" buffet. There are plenty of games and contests (many of which involve taking off your clothes), along with dancing and plenty of drinking. Make sure to wear your Sunday best for Bullshit Bingo, in which a cow is walked around big numbered squares until she unleashes a steaming pile of you-know-what. There's also a wet T-shirt contest for women and a hairy chest contest for the guys. Another favorite is the "Bite the Ball" Motorcycle Ride, where bikers and their passengers attempt to ride by and bite a hanging bull testicle.

During the weekend, you'll probably saddle up on Ol' Testy, the life-size 900-pound wooden bull with massive testicles that is rolled into the middle of the lodge's bar. Be warned that those who climb aboard for a photo-op are "encouraged" to remove some clothing, as well as engage in another Testicle Festival tradition. "Everyone wants

to touch Ol' Testy's nuts," Rod claims. "It's kind of like kissing the Blarney Stone."

Rod Lincoln

There are many rumors about the strange and sometimes mystical healing powers attributed to a bull's testicles. Some say they act as an aphrodisiac. Others claim that rubbing these deep-fried goodies on your baby's head will lead it to a healthy and plentiful life. Whatever the results of the Testicle Festival, you'll definitely find ample reason to be amused, delighted, or revolted.

When You Go:

Undoubtedly, you'll be sampling some gonads at the Testicle Festival. Brave souls have described the chewy experience as "like chicken or veal," "slippery like liver or gizzards," and "like rubber bands dipped in formaldehyde." The "official" recipe calls for soaking them in brine, then adding some secret spices and a beer marinade. Next, they're put through a special cooling system to dehydrate them. Then, the testicles are quadruple-breaded in a wet-dry batter and deep fried.

Web Coordinate:

www.whatsgoingon.com/100things/testicle

"the bawdiest and most absurd festival in the USA"

Burning Man Project

Black Rock Desert, Nevada, USA

GPS Lat: 39.24912 N Lon: 114.87792 W

Neopagan. Postapocalyptic. Nouveau hippie. Ordered anarchy. Radical self-expression. Temporary autonomy. These are just a few of the catchy terms used to describe the otherwise intangible Burning Man Project. The *Village Voice* described this Labor Day Weekend circus in the Black Rock Desert of northern

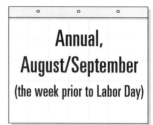

**Annual,
August/September**
(the week prior to Labor Day)

Nevada as ". . . a guerrilla war against the commodification of the collective imagination." Wow! Where do we sign up?!

In 1986, on the heels of a messy break up, Larry Harvey burned a wooden effigy of his ex with friends on the last weekend of summer. What started out as a neat-o way to bring closure to a soured relationship has evolved into an ongoing "project" that brings together artists, performers, techies, ravers, and deviants from all over the world in a so-called "experiment in a temporary community." Over 12,000 revelers show up for the spectacle. Nude acrobats, paragliding, mock celebrity crucifixions, toilet surfing, and a drive-by shooting gallery are just some of the oddities and activities you might run across. And remember, no one is a spectator at Burning Man—everyone is a participant!

For this massive communal experience, the desert is temporarily transformed into Black Rock City, with sub-villages, public transit, and communal cooking areas. You'll have to choose from—or make your own—theme camps to reside in, so like-minded participants, or "Burners," can reside and play together. Theme camps run the gamut of ideas and ideologies. With specialized themes like the Free Mass Shower camp, the Costco Soulmate Outfit, and the Guns and Ammo camp, you're sure to find one that fits your bill. Burners can camp or sleep in their cars, but motorized vehicular traffic is strictly limited.

During the day there are plenty of activities—scheduled and spontaneous—to keep you feeling like part of the community. A variety of musical acts, dances, and performance art spectacles spring up on impromptu stages.

Then there's the Burning Man himself. This 50-foot wooden stick figure, stuffed with fireworks and neon lights, gets torched as the finale of the week of celebration. At dusk, a "Burning Pageant" winds through the camps and ends up at the Burning Man. The crowd swells around crying, "Burn him! Burn him!" as the flames begin to shoot up his legs and arms. What does it all mean? The decline of civilization? The hope for renewal? Who really cares? The Burning Man stands for whatever you want him to stand for.

Copyright 1998 Margot Duane

When You Go:

You must take your own shelter, food, and water (at least one gallon per person per day is recommended). Consider packing a parachute or tarp to put up for shade. If you are sleeping in your car, you can cover it with the parachute at night. Take plenty of sunscreen and a jacket; the temperature can range from over 100 degrees in the day to near freezing at night. Children are allowed; however, dogs are forbidden. Admission tickets are required and can be purchased in advance.

Web Coordinate:

www.whatsgoingon.com/ 100things/burningman

"an ongoing 'project' that brings together artists, performers, techies, ravers, and deviants"

National Finals Rodeo

Thomas and Mack Arena, Las Vegas, Nevada, USA

GPS Lat: 36.20575 N Lon: 115.22279 W

It's the roughest, toughest, and richest expression of a uniquely American sport. Yes, it's the annual National Finals Rodeo, and it happens every December in . . . Las Vegas. That's right, Vegas, baby. Chips and cow chips all in the same place.

Annual, December

Thousands of rodeos take place each year all over America, but the Finals is the last stop on the circuit. Over one hundred of rodeo's most talented compete for the largest purse in the sport, which at last count was over $4 million. The action takes place at the enormous Thomas and Mack Arena. There are more than ten rounds, and, in true Vegas fashion, each round of the rodeo has a payoff to the winner. At the end of the rodeo, the participant who has won the most rounds also wins the "average payoff," which is the largest prize at the National Finals Rodeo.

Whether you envy the independent, no-bosses life of the rodeo cowboy, or you cling to the notion that cowboys are the true embodiment of the fading American dream, or you simply like to drink beer and laugh like an idiot whenever someone bites the dust, the Finals is always a hoot. It offers the utmost in a sport already filled with excitement, danger, extraordinary skill, and the most rugged of rugged individuals.

City slickers may not be familiar with how it works, so here's a rundown. Pro rodeo consists of two types of events: roughstock events and timed events. In the roughstock events—bareback riding, saddle bronc riding, and bull riding—a contestant's score depends equally on his performance and how the animal performs, or how the beast jumps and bucks. In order to get a high score, the cowboy or cowgirl, while using only one hand, must stay aboard the bucking horse or bull for eight seconds. If riders touch the animal with their

free hand, they're disqualified. In the timed events—calf roping and steer roping—a competitor's goal is to wrassle or rope that sucker as quickly as possible.

Every sport has superstars, and rodeo is no exception. In recent years, athletes like Ty Murray ("The King of the Cowboys") and Kristie Peterson have injected even more adrenaline into this already exciting sport. Murray was the youngest cowboy ever to win the PRCA all-around championship in 1989, at age nineteen, and he has broken many records since then. Unusual for rodeo stars, he rides in all three rough-stock events—during the same competition! Peterson and her horse, Bozo, have been the tops in barrel racing. She's a former school bus driver who's won many National Finals titles since 1993.

> "the roughest, toughest, and richest expression of a uniquely American sport"

When You Go:

A smattering of other cowboy-style events happen around the National Finals Rodeo. Check out the Wrangler Best Fittin' Jeans Contest and Line Dance or the Miss Rodeo Pageant to get into the spirit. Every afternoon at the Cowboy Christmas Gift Show, you can rub shoulders with your favorite rodeo stars. If you can't get tickets to the Finals, remember that the events are simulcast via closed-circuit to many of the hotels along the Strip.

Web Coordinate:

www.whatsgoingon.com/100things/rodeo

Photo courtesy of Professional Rodeo Cowboys Association

Roswell UFO Encounter

Roswell, New Mexico, USA

GPS Lat: 33.38333 N Lon: 104.51666 W

New Mexico, land of enchantment. Site of the first atomic bomb explosion. Home of Smokey the Bear. And in 1947, some say, the location of an alien encounter when an unidentified object crashed on Hub Corn's sheep ranch and caused quite a stir. Every year, "Roswellians" descend on and double

Annual, July
(first week)

the population of Roswell, New Mexico, for the Roswell UFO Encounter festival. It's all to celebrate the intellectual and the inane, in America's biggest gathering of UFOlogists, alien abductees, conspiracy theorists, true believers, skeptics, and lovers of kitsch.

On the night of July 8, 1947, an unidentified flying object crashed on ranchland 20 miles north of Roswell. The government reported that the fallen "disk" was a spaceship. Days later, the government retracted its statement and said that what had actually crashed was a weather balloon. The story changed again in 1997, when the government stated that the debris was from a top-secret spy balloon.

The shroud of mystery surrounding this suspicious event has sparked endless debate and flights of fancy. Was the object a weather balloon, a spy satellite, or a flying saucer filled with little silver men, who might or might not have died on impact, and who were whisked away to the local air base to be autopsied (as many contend), all to become just another one of our government's dirty little secrets?

You'll hear all about it at the Roswell UFO Encounter. Attend the UFO lecture series on alien breeding experiments and alien autopsies; the UFO Trade Show with alien belt buckles, alien shirts, and aliens in a jar; a Galactic Grand Prix parade of homemade spaceships; a Flying Saucer (pancake) Eating Contest; and even a production of *Roswell, the Musical.* You'll be busy with the Alien Village's food stands and crafts vendors, the pageantry of the Alien Costume Con-

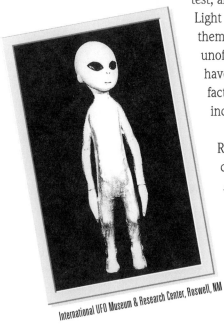

International UFO Museum & Research Center, Roswell, NM

test, and the splendor of the Laser and Light Shows. Check out two (count them: two!) UFO museums, official and unofficial UFO crash sites, and if you have time, stop by the huge mozzarella factory that is Roswell's other source of income.

So get into the spirit and head for Roswell, because no USA road trip is complete without a glimpse of America's obsession with the paranormal. There's no better place to witness it than Roswell, where you get the added bonus of seeing thousands of freakers.

When You Go:

Roswell is equally accessible to humans and aliens, as in addition to cornfields, it boasts its own airport. It's hot as heck in New Mexico in July, so don't forget your sunglasses, sunblock, and bottles of water. Fill your fanny pack with cash, because Roswell residents charge for just about everything. Besides, you'll want to stock up on plenty of alien beef jerky and outer space bumper stickers, because this is an experience you won't want to forget.

> "America's biggest gathering of UFOlogists, alien abductees, conspiracy theorists, true believers, skeptics, and lovers of kitsch"

Web coordinate:

www.whatsgoingon.com/100things/UFO

Greenwich Village Halloween Parade

Greenwich Village, New York City, New York, USA

GPS Lat: 40.66980 N Lon: 073.94384 W

Greenwich Village is always a great place to find a good freak show, but there's one night that's the best, when "normal" people get demented and freaks get freakier. The Village trans-forms into the ultimate costume party on October 31 for the nation's largest and most exuberant Halloween celebra-tion.

Annual, October 31

Over 20,000 costumed civilians, dancers, musicians, and other exhibitionists parade up Sixth Avenue on Halloween night. It's mainly for their own benefit, but it entertains the 1.5 million people who gather there to watch, too.

As only New York can do it, the Village Halloween Parade is the most enthusiastic and craziest collection of costumed misfits and rev-eling rogues you can imagine. On this night, the distinction between society's rejects and social climbers dissolves into a swirl of Carniva-lesque mayhem. New Yorkers forget that they can't stand each other and embrace the diversity that makes the city great.

Ghosts, witches, goblins, skeletons, monsters, dragons, and a fair share of Freddie Kreugers mingle with more creative, off-the-wall cre-ations like slices of toast, boxes of Chinese take-out, and abstract art. What is unique about the parade is not the latest in American pop culture, wacky drag queens, or clever headline rip-offs (though that's definitely part of the fun); every year, organizers commission special puppets to lead the parade. The results are spectacular creations that seem to float through the air, usually operated by two to three people.

There's just as much to see on the sidelines of the parade, so pick-ing a spot to watch is serious business. Spectators pack the streets, pushing against police barricades, standing on cars, and climbing atop telephone booths. The veterans go early to apartment parties or restaurants and plant themselves at open windows that overlook the chaos.

42

The whole thing began in 1973 as a neighborhood walk with puppeteer Ralph Lee and his children. It has since won countless awards and grants for its economic and cultural contribution to New York City. In 1994, the mayor issued a proclamation that said, "The Village Halloween Parade presents the single greatest opportunity for ALL New Yorkers to exhibit their creativity in an event that is one-of-a-kind, unique and memorable every year." You can deal with that.

When You Go:

It's in New York City. If you can't find it, you're living in a vacuum. Be prepared for all kinds of weather, since this time of year is pretty unpredictable. To march, just show up at Sixth Avenue between Spring and Canal Streets in costume. Spectators, take note: it's usually packed from Bleeker to Fourteenth Streets, so if you're not a people person, pick a spot at the beginning or end of the parade. For scary Halloween action later, the Village is the perfect place.

Web coordinate:

www.whatsgoingon.com/100things/greenwich

Danielle Kiesler

43

New Year's Eve in Times Square

Times Square, New York City, New York, USA

GPS Lat: 40.78333 N Lon: 073.96666 W

As the curtain closes on another year, the most intense place to watch it happen is Times Square, in the heart of New York City. Where else can you belt out "Auld Lang Syne" with half a million people?

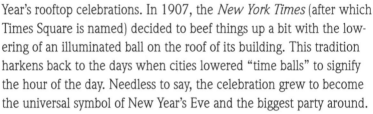

**Annual,
December 31**

Back in 1904, the owners of One Times Square began conducting New Year's rooftop celebrations. In 1907, the *New York Times* (after which Times Square is named) decided to beef things up a bit with the lowering of an illuminated ball on the roof of its building. This tradition harkens back to the days when cities lowered "time balls" to signify the hour of the day. Needless to say, the celebration grew to become the universal symbol of New Year's Eve and the biggest party around.

Over 300 million television viewers tune their sets to the Ball Lowering, and over 500,000 come out to watch it live—that's more than six football stadiums full of people in the streets! With so many people vying for the best spot to brave the cold New York air, smart revelers get to Times Square early. Mittens and thermoses filled with hot chocolate are recommended.

At 6:00 P.M., the New Year's Eve Ball is in its highest position on the flagpole. All 500 pounds of the 6-foot-in-diameter ball are ready to be lit. One hundred eighty 75-watt halogen lamps, 144 glitter strobe lights, a powerful 10,000-watt internal xenon lamp, and 12,000 large rhinestones make for one bright ball! At 6 P.M., the halogen lamps on the exterior of the ball are illuminated into various patterns that change every second while glitter strobes flash randomly. If you are prone to flashbacks and strange attacks, look away!

After a few hours of mindless conversation with strangers, a few trips to any business kind enough to let you use their bathroom, and six hours of blinding lights and inane musical acts, you're ready for action. Some sort of special guest (flavor of the year) joins a government official to push the button that lowers the ball. As the last few seconds of the year become the past, the anticipation is unbearable.

After the clock strikes midnight, the ball drops, 3,500 pounds of confetti and giant balloons are released, fireworks go off—and all of a sudden you feel very close to 500,000 strangers. The next thing you know, you're smooching your neighbor, singing off key, and living and loving life.

Times Square BID/Dana F. Holway

No other New Year's Eve celebration can possibly compare. After more than ninety years of throwing the world's biggest bash, you know they're doing something right!

When You Go:

Take along a whole lot of patience and a sense of humor. Frigid cold weather and thousands of people can really test the old nerves. If you need a way to spend the first half of your day, get tickets for a matinee performance of a Broadway show. (It's warm in there!) A cheaper option may be catching a peep show at any area sex shop still in operation. (It's *really* warm in there!) C'mon, you're in New York City—you'll find something to do!

Web Coordinate:

www.whatsgoingon.com/100things/timessquare

> "the universal symbol of New Year's Eve and the biggest party around"

National Hollerin' Contest

Midway High School, Spivey's Corner, North Carolina, USA

GPS Lat: 35.18333 N Lon: 078.48333 W

Warm up them vocal chords for the National Hollerin' Contest in Spivey's Corner, North Carolina, the "Hollerin'" Capital of the Universe." The Spivey's Corner Volunteer Fire Department hosts the most unusual and resounding of all vocal competitions every year.

Annual, June
(third Saturday)

Imagine a time with no telephones, radios, automobiles, or daily papers, when mail came about two or three times a week. In the flat open plains of North Carolina, hollerin' became a way of life and served for communication over long distances to family, neighbors, and animals who were often a mile or so away. There were hollers to bring in the cows, the hogs, and the huntin' dogs; to say "I'm awake, and all is well today"; to get your kids to bring you water; to say "time to eat"; to greet; and to announce your approach to someone else's property. There was also a "get help" distress holler.

Times have changed, but the hollerin' tradition continues. In 1969, in response to concerns about the dying hollerin' breed, the Hollerin' Contest was inaugurated, and 5,000 people showed up. Today, the National Hollerin' Contest is internationally known, and many winners have appeared on national television.

Hollerin', rural North Carolina style, sounds a little like yodelin', a little like screamin', a little like singin', and a little like yellin'. They say your holler expresses your mood and is as distinctive as your face. There is a long history of both melodic and practical calls being used by ranchers, farmers, hunters, and workers the world over, including in California, the Philippines, Haiti, Nigeria, Cuba, Burma, India, Austria, and Ecuador. But the eastern North Carolina style of hollerin' is unique.

At Spivey's Corner, contest day is filled with lots of down-home activities, cooking, and music, all leading up to the competitions. First is a Whistlin' Contest, followed by Conch Shell and Fox Horn Blowin' contests. Then, hollerers age twelve and under compete in the Junior Hollerin' Contest, followed by the Ladies Callin' Contest, and finally the main event, the National Hollerin' Contest.

Photo by Janice L. Edwards

Spivey's Corner may seem like a rural outpost where you won't fit in, but don't be intimidated. The locals will welcome you—and maybe even your voice—with open arms, and a hollerin' good time can be shared by all. So warm up those vocal chords, drink lots of hot tea with honey and lemon, gargle some salt water, and make your way down to the hollerin' capital of the universe to join the action.

When You Go:

On contest day, there's also a Greased Pole climbing competition for kids and a Watermelon Roll for their parents (during which the fire department tries to knock contestants over with water sprayed from a fire hose). For lunch, the fire department prepares barbecue pork, grilled chicken, fries, burgers, and hot

> "the most unusual and resounding of all vocal competitions"

dogs. There is live bluegrass, country, and gospel music most of the day. The closest airport to Spivey's Corner is Raleigh-Durham International Airport, which is still about a hundred miles away.

Web Coordinate:

www.whatsgoingon.com/100things/hollerin

47

World Cow Chip Throwing Championship

Beaver Fairgrounds Arena, Beaver, Oklahoma, USA

GPS Lat: 36.81666 N Lon: 100.51666 W

Annual, April
(third weekend)

Call it what you will—crap, doodie, chips, poop, manure, excrement, caca—when you pick it up and fling it, you can't help but think of those esteemed poop-pitching athletes who blazed the trail before you. The World Cow Chip Throwing Championship is the most eccentric—and smelliest—contest of them all. It is for anyone who ever had a dream to be the best, to be number two. Uh, number one.

Back in the 1800s, the settlers of the Oklahoma prairie faced serious conditions, with a scarcity of water, extreme weather, and the lack of timber for fuel and shelter. They were often in dire need of cooking and heating fuel during the severe winters on the open plains.

The settlers soon discovered that dried buffalo dung burned extremely well. But the buffalo were almost extinct. So every fall, the settlers steered their wagons to the pastures and loaded up on cow chips for the winter. It wasn't as clean burning, but it was still a life-saver. As entire families flung the bovine doo-doo into the wagons, somehow the job transformed into a competition.

Cut to Beaver, Oklahoma, 1970. Rules are instituted, and the World Cow Chip Throwing Championship formally begins. Contestants are allowed two chips each, which they select from a pile provided on a wagon. The chip thrown the farthest counts. Chips must be at least 6 inches in diameter. If competitors shape them in any way, there's a 25-foot penalty. If the doodie breaks up in mid-air, the piece that travels the farthest counts. "Chippers" must be at least sixteen years old.

Photo by Brent Lansden

Throwing style plays an important role in cow chip throwing. Some chippers use the underhanded softball pitch approach. Others fling the dung like a Frisbee or heave it like a shot put. Leland Searcy chucked a chip 182 feet 3 inches in 1979, setting the standard for shooting the shit. As the competition has grown, competitors have traveled from all fifty states in the USA and a few foreign countries.

During all this competitive fun, don't forget those who suffered through the harsh winters on the prairie, those fabled first few who pitched their dung into the wagons. Their spirits will be with you. As will be the flies.

When You Go:

There are many other events during the week of the Cow Chip Throwing in the Beaver County Cimarron Territory Celebration. Check out the chili cook-offs, craft shows, stock car races, talent shows, and helicopter rides. To get to Beaver, you'll likely have to drive about 150 miles from Amarillo, Texas. In case you want to keep warm by burning manure, remember that beef cattle manure provides 6,400 BTUs per pound. Pig manure is not as efficient, at 5,000 BTUs (and it's also the smelliest).

> "the most eccentric—and smelliest—contest of them all"

Web Coordinate:

www.whatsgoingon.com/100things/cowchip

Mangum Rattlesnake Derby

Mangum, Oklahoma, USA

GPS Lat: 34.87878 N Lon: 099.50136 W

The Mangum Rattlesnake Derby offers a chance to overcome your deepest anxieties while participating in a unique slice of Americana. You'll come face-to-face with more venomous, slithering rattlesnakes than you have ever seen in one place—even in your scariest nightmares. Indeed, rattlesnakes have a bad reputation and can be dangerous, but they are actually quite reclusive and probably more afraid of you than you are of them!

Annual, April
(third weekend)

The Derby brings about 30,000 people to downtown Mangum. At the southwest corner of the main square, hundreds of rattlers are displayed in open-air pits that you can approach within inches and still be perfectly safe. You can even get your picture taken with a new, fang-laden pal wrapped around your neck.

Nearby, under the red-and-white striped tent, professional snake handlers host the continuous "Snake Pit Show," starring rattlesnakes and pythons, alligators, and other exotic critters. When you've experienced enough live action, you can head over to the Butcher Shop Show, on South Oklahoma Street, and learn how rattlesnakes are processed for food, leather, and medicine. And yes, they do taste like chicken—but you need to cook an entire snake to get a decent meal.

Bus tours leave every hour on the hour to observe live rattlesnakes in the wild. Members of the Mangum Rattlesnake Association lead the excursions and relate all the myths and facts about these incredible (and misunderstood) creatures.

If you're really interested in overcoming old anxieties, experienced guides provide the proper equipment and training, then lead you down to the hunting areas where the slithery creatures reside. If you are lucky, you may walk away with a cash prize in the Derby Competition for the "Largest Snake," "Most Pounds of Snakes," or

"Most Snakes" categories. The Derby's "Fangmaster" presides over the competition.

Rattlesnake derbies and roundups happen in rural towns all over the South and Southwest, but the spectacle in Mangum is one of the most picturesque and authentic. From the days of the Oklahoma Territory, ranchers and farmers around Mangum have controlled the

> "a chance to overcome your deepest anxieties while participating in a unique slice of Americana"

rattlesnake populations on their land with organized hunts. Today, animal rights activists claim that events like the Derby are cruel and unnecessary, but the good folks of Mangum say it is part of their heritage and just good fun. See for yourself.

When You Go:

If you have no interest in rattlesnakes, don't fret. There is "something for everyone" at Derby Weekend. The flea market includes more than 500 dealers, plus about one hundred vendors serving up all kinds of food. Be sure to sample the southern-fried rattlesnake. Stick around for the "crowning moment" of the Derby, when the "Miss Derby Princess" takes the throne and poses with the award winners and their record snakes.

Web Coordinate:

www.whatsgoingon.com/100things/rattlesnake

Mangum Shortgrass Rattlesnake Assn.

Battle of Gettysburg Reenactment

Gettysburg, Pennsylvania, USA

GPS Lat: 39.81666 N Lon: 077.21666 W

The Battle of Gettysburg was the grand-daddy of all Civil War battles. On its anniversary each year, during Fourth of July weekend, it is recreated in what has become the USA's biggest military flash-back. Gettysburg was so important and was the site of so much carnage that it has captured the imaginations of school-

Annual, July

(Fourth of July weekend)

children and war buffs for over a century. The reenactment allows 20,000 people to participate each year. Many more watch, learn, and have a great deal of fun.

By the time of the battle in 1863, the Civil War had been in progress for two years, and no end was in sight. General Robert E. Lee moved his Confederate troops north into Pennsylvania to turn up the heat a little. The Battle of Gettysburg started by chance when a Confederate supply brigade ran into the Union army.

Over three days, 172,000 soldiers fought and about 45,000 became casualties (killed, wounded, captured, or missing). Five thou-sand horses were killed. The Union won the battle during the South's failed Pickett's Charge. There were 10,000 casualties in just fifty min-utes in this attack—more than three per second! (The fighting was so intense that bullets heading toward each other often collided and fused in midair! Visitors to Gettysburg's National Military Park Visi-tors Center can see such bullets.) A Confederate victory could have meant a different outcome of the Civil War.

During the three-day reenactment, many actual skirmishes are replayed. Anyone sixteen or older can apply to become a soldier (thir-teen or older for musicians). There are many units to choose from, such as infantry, cavalry, artillery, and fife and drum. You can take your own horse, but it must be used to the noise of gunshots. (Don't worry—blanks are used!)

The Battle of Gettysburg Reenactment is intense and loud. Every day there is a gigantic cannon barrage. Musket volleys, the smell of powder, and the thundering of hooves are everywhere. The battle reenactment usually ends with a re-creation of Pickett's Charge. Throughout the battle, authenticity is ensured by strict rules (for example, muskets must be correct for the period).

> "the USA's biggest military flashback"

Also fun during the three days of the reenactment are a Civil War wedding, period religious services, medical shows, Civil War music, a field hospital, and a weapons show. Vendors in period costumes set up their wares in white hospital tents to sell authentic clothing, weapons, food, and collectibles. Whether your preference is fighting, playing music, watching, buying, or eating, you're sure to have a great time and even learn something about this bloody event in American history.

When You Go:

The reenactment takes place on a 300-acre field mobbed with spectators and reenactors. Traffic before and after is terrible. You must pay to enter. The line to view the battle is over three-quarters of a mile long, and only limited seating is available (at an extra charge). If you take a kid five or fewer years old with you, explain what will happen ahead of time, as young children sometimes freak at the loud cannon noises. No pets are allowed.

Web Coordinate:

www.whatsgoingon.com/100things/gettysburg

Courtesy of George Lomas

Art Car Weekend

Houston, Texas, USA

GPS Lat: 29.76870 N Lon: 095.38672 W

Annual, mid-April

Every year, artists from California to Canada speed their mobile masterpieces down freeways and back roads toward Houston, Texas, for a celebration of creativity and America's love affair with the automobile. They're there for Art Car Weekend, a one-of-a-kind, all-out homage to a uniquely American art form. It all started in the 1980s, with art car pioneers like local artist Jackie Harris, who encrusted her car with plastic fruit, and performance artist Gene Pool, who spread seeds on his car and grew a thick carpet of grass. Considering its eccentricity and major dependence on automobiles, Houston is the perfect place to see these rolling art galleries.

Over 200 decorated, augmented, and embellished vehicles and "rolling sculptures" strut their stuff in the Art Car Parade on Saturday. Art car enthusiasts are diverse—low riders, junior high school students, trained artists, and just plain folks. All you need is a car, a vision, and the guts to drive your work of art around town. As if the amazing autos weren't enough, the parade is punctuated with throngs of bikers, roller bladers, drag queens, and musicians. Over 250,000 people crowd the sidewalks each year, so get there early.

Past parades have offered a selection of bizarre vehicles that boggle the mind. Visionaries include art car "Da Vinci" David Best, who pastes vacuum cleaners and Virgins of Guadaloupe on his car; rolling art guru Larry Fuente, whose "Cowasaki," a decorated Kawasaki motorcycle straddled by a stuffed cow, pioneered art cars; and art car legend Harrod Blank, who covers his van with cameras that actually work. Blank uses them to photograph people's reactions to his car.

The Art Car Symposium covers issues related to the art car genre. The famous, outrageous Art Car Ball draws over 4,500 revelers to the

roof of the Allright Parking Garage. There, you can marvel at many of the art cars close up, chat with their creators, and feast on fab food. Houston's hottest bands entertain, and attendees have even gotten married at Eternal Combustion's short-term McMarriage booth in a ceremony involving holy water and spraying for demons.

The Art Car Weekend is organized by the Orange Show Foundation, as part of the Houston International Festival. The foundation is committed to "encouraging the extraordinary artistic expressions of ordinary people"—but from the looks of Art Car Weekend, there is nothing ordinary about it!

When You Go:

No need for your cowboy hat and boots; Houston's pretty cosmopolitan. What you do need is a car to get around, since public transportation's not so good. Take lots of water and light clothes, as it gets hot and very humid in Houston. Be prepared for rain (don't paste any water solubles on your car). To enter, contact the Orange Show Foundation; with the growing popularity of the parade, entrants must register, and not all are accepted. Stop by the Art Car Museum if you get the notion.

> "a celebration of creativity and America's love affair with the automobile"

Web coordinate:

www.whatsgoingon.com/100things/artcar

SPAMARAMA

Auditorium Shores, Austin, Texas, USA

GPS Lat: 30.26666 N Lon: 097.73333 W

Cook-offs are an American institution—and so is eccentricity. It was only a matter of time before the two got together, and the result is the SPAMARAMA, the oddest and most (un)savory cook-off in America. Chefs from around the country travel to Austin, Texas, every year to try to make that gooey potted pork product, SPAM, into a tasty dish.

Annual, April/May

The two founders of the SPAMARAMA, Dick Terry and David Arnsberger, thought of the event in 1978 while discussing the virtues of a prominent Texan tradition—the chili cook-off. Terry mused, "Anyone can cook chili. . . . Now if someone could make SPAM edible, that would be a challenge. We ought to have a SPAM-Off." And they went through with it.

Decades later, they're still going at it—with more corny SPAM slogans than ever—and hordes of people are actually forking over the five bucks to get into this pork party. "When we started this thing in 1978, we had no idea that 10,000 people would come out to witness its spectacularness twenty years later," says Arnsberger. "It was kind of like a fun event for a few years, to go out and get a beer, but it started to get real popular. It receives local, national, even worldwide attendance."

Several events lie at the center of the SPAMARAMA. In addition to the SPAM cook-off, a SPAM Jam features local bands, many performing SPAM parodies. SPAM lovers vie against each other in the SPAMalympics, with the Pork Pull (a tug-of-war over a pool of SPAM jelly), the SPAM toss, the SPAM call, the SPAM relay, and the SPAM CRAM, a SPAM-burger eating contest (and perhaps afterward, an unauthorized SPAM throwing up in the bathroom event).

Meanwhile, with the SPAMerica's Cup at stake, chefs try to make the potted meat into a tasty dish. Some notable dishes from past SPAMA-RAMAs include SPAMbalaya and SPAM-stuffed jalapeños. Understandably boozed-up local celebrity judges sample the SPAMmy dishes.

United Cerebral Palsy Association of the Capitol Area, Inc.

Taste isn't the only thing that the SPAMbitious cooks are shooting for. Two other categories are as important, and more intriguing: Showmanship and Worst. Showmanship winners have included a carving of a pig's ass out of SPAM and a detailed carving of a rat. For Worst, SPAMARAMA legend Pops Conway enters (every year!) a cheesy mayonnaise- and raisin-loaded SPAM dish called SPAMish Fly. Sounds delicious!

When You Go:

Get to work on creating a tasty recipe (hint: try to use as little SPAM and as much of other ingredients as possible). Training for the SPAMalympics can't be difficult, but keep the TUMS close-by when beefing up on SPAM-burgers. Before you go, watch the Monty Python skit "The Final Rip-Off" (available on video), which will help you get into the

> "the oddest and most (un)savory cook-off in America"

spirit with the song "SPAM, SPAM, lovely SPAM." At the cook-off, look out for *SPAMARAMA: The Cookbook*, featuring winning recipes, a historical perspective, and artwork.

Web Coordinate:

www.whatsgoingon.com/100things/spamarama

Calgary Stampede and Exhibition

Stampede Park, Calgary, Alberta, Canada

GPS Lat: 51.08333 N Lon: 114.08333 W

The year was 1912 when a trick roper by the name of Guy Weadick found Calgary a suitable home for the cowboy shenanigans now called the Calgary Stampede. His dream was to create a spectacle that would "make Buffalo Bill's Wild West Extravaganza look like a side show."

Annual, July

To date, over a billion people have attended the event called "The Greatest Outdoor Show on Earth," and no one has yet to challenge the title. This rowdy show of Canadian cowboy culture takes place every summer, and for ten days the usually cosmopolitan Calgary morphs back to its cow-town roots.

The main attraction during the Stampede is the nightly "Range-land Derby" Chuckwagon Races, known to locals as simply "The Chucks." Billed as a "sport straight from the pages of Western history," chuckwagon races are said to have originated in the cattle drives of the 1800s, when chuckwagon drivers would race ahead of their outfits in order to find the best campsites. These lumbering mobile kitchens served as the rangeland dining rooms and social centers for generations of cowboys. At the Stampede, fully equipped wooden wagons are manned by four "outriders" and pulled by teams of four thoroughbred horses. They race in heats in a dangerously tight figure-eight configuration for a $500,000 (Canadian) winner-take-all prize.

During the afternoons, you can watch some of the best rodeo around. You'll see steer wrestlers, calf ropers, and bull riders all risking their lives and vying for huge cash prizes. In addition, there are some unique events like wild cow milking and a wild horse race.

There are plenty of other Western oddities to entertain you at the Stampede. For example, check out the Hogs and Logs event, where pigs, ducks, and roosters all race around the track together. Or stop by the Lumberjack Show, which features log rolling, saw races, and double-bladed axe throwing.

> "a rowdy show of Canadian cowboy culture"

Saunter down Main Street of the recreated Wild West town complete with a casino and criminals. An authentic First Nations encampment features a teepee-raising contest, pow wow, tribal dances, bead-work demonstrations, hide preparation, and traditional games. Thrill rides and agricultural and livestock exhibits round out the Stampede attractions.

Exciting world-famous (primarily Canadian) entertainers will have you singin' all the way home to your range.

When You Go:

As you can imagine, the Chuckwagon Races are the toughest ticket at the Stampede, and the event is always sold out weeks in advance. After you see the Chucks, stick around for the nightly fireworks finale. There are also special, discounted two-day packages that include tickets to the Rodeo Show and Chuckwagon Races and admission to all attractions at Stampede Park.

Web Coordinate:

www.whatsgoingon.com/100things/stampede

Courtesy of the Calgary Stampede

Latin America and the Caribbean

The Monarch Butterfly Migration

Junkanoo

Saut d'Eau Vodou Pilgrimage

Vernal Equinox at Chichen Itza

Día de los Muertos

Los Diablos Danzantes

Semana Santa

La Fiesta de la Virgen de la Candelaria

Carnaval

Reveillon Rio

Argentine Polo Finals

Argentine Polo Finals (Campeonato Argentino Abierto)

Campo de Polo, Palermo, Buenos Aires, Argentina

GPS Lat: 34.40000 S Lon: 058.50000 W

Annual, December
(first Saturday)

It is believed that polo was invented over 2,000 years ago in Persia. But the Argentines can take credit for transforming the game into the gritty and glitzy spectacle it is today.

For the past century, Argentina has dominated international polo, effortlessly producing more championship players and teams than any other country. The sport is a national obsession, and there is no better place to witness this than at the Campeonato Argentino Abierto. Even though the Abierto is a national championship, it's considered the premier polo event on the planet.

Over 15,000 people watch the match at the Campo de Polo in Buenos Aires's affluent Palermo district. Locals (called *portenos*) also refer to the Campo as "The Cathedral of Polo." Many of the spectators need only step out of their high-rise apartment and walk a few blocks to watch the action.

The final match is typically held on the first Saturday in December. Eight professional, four-man teams play qualifying matches in the weeks prior to the first Saturday in December to determine which teams will play in the final game.

Polo is played on a huge turf field that is the size of about nine football fields (160 × 300 yards). The fast-moving play takes place over the entire field, so every seat offers a good view of the match.

The entire match takes about ninety minutes to complete, and the actual playing time is divided into six seven-minute periods, called "chuckers." Each player has six fully equipped thoroughbred horses at the ready, one for each chucker (it's no wonder that polo is considered the ultimate rich man's sport!). The horses are bred specifically for polo and are typically between five and fifteen years old.

Corbis/Paul A. Souders

It has been said that to play polo one must ride like a warrior, think like a chess player, and hit like a golf pro while your opponents try to break your kneecaps. This "gentlemanly" sport can often get quite rough, with players hooking opponents' mallets, stealing balls, and running opponents off course.

As with many spectator sports, one of the best parts of the Abierto is the people watching. The crowd is a reserved and well-dressed mix of affluent *portenos*, local celebrities, and international jet setters. Around the field are concession stands and stalls selling luxury goods and polo gear. And at halftime (between the third and fourth chuckers) spectators are encouraged to soil their Gucci loafers and Prada stilettos by stepping out on the field and stomping the divots back into the ground.

When You Go:

Tickets are tough to get for the final game of Abierto; it might be easier to score tickets to one of the qualifying matches. The final match usually begins around 5 P.M. Expect temperate, spring-like weather. And if you see the game locally on television, you'll probably be surprised that it is broadcast with minimal play-by-play commentary. Evidently, Argentines regard this as a distraction and would prefer to hear only the sounds of the hoofs and the mallets.

Web Coordinate:

www.whatsgoingon.com/100things/polo

> "the premier polo event on the planet"

La Fiesta de la Virgen de la Candelaria

Copacabana, Bolivia

GPS Lat: 16.18333 S Lon: 069.11666 W

Twelve thousand feet high in the Andes between Peru and Bolivia is the immense Lake Titicaca. This region has always been holy. Before the Spaniards brought Catholicism in the mid-1500s, Incan rituals were a strong element in the lifestyle of the inhabitants. On February 2 each year, there is a high-altitude

Annual, February 2

explosion of color, sound, entertainment, and religious ceremony during the Fiesta de la Virgen de la Candelaria, a Christian-Indian celebration in Copacabana, a town of 5,000 on a peninsula jutting into Lake Titicaca.

As you might guess, the Fiesta de la Virgen de la Candelaria has a mixed ethnic flavor in Copacabana. The Fiesta centers around the town's white Moorish-style cathedral, and the entire town comes alive. Several days before February 2, Indians from the countryside start arriving. The town is decorated colorfully, and people play music and dance everywhere. Fortune-tellers, merchants, and charlatans set up shop. People are blessed and prayers are chanted all over town, especially in the main square.

The fiesta comes from the historic connection among the Virgin, Copacabana, and Incan heritage. Near Copacabana are two highly revered islands, Isla del Sol and Isla de la Luna, where the Incans believe the world began. There is also a strong Christian tradition. In the late 1500s, a grandson of an Incan emperor said he saw an apparition of the Virgin Mary in Copacabana. Then a statue of the Virgin was brought to Copacabana. (Candelaria, or Candlemas, is celebrated throughout the Christian world. It is the day the Virgin Mary was purified after the birth of Jesus.) Since that time, both the Virgin and the day of Candelaria have become pivotal to both the Christian and Indian religions in Copacabana.

Religious strength has turned Copacabana into a bazaar of religion. For example, people drive from all over Bolivia to the town square to have their vehicles blessed by Franciscan priests. Incan religious practices still thrive as well. People bury llama fetuses under their homes and splash sugary alcoholic beverages on their foundations to bring protection and good luck.

During the fiesta, celebrants beat drums and perform traditional Indian dances and mock bullfights. There is a grand religious procession, which includes a duplicate of the statue of the Virgin. In addition, the conquest of the Incas by Pizarro is reenacted by local Indians, but with a pro-Indian twist—the slain Incan king comes back to life (just like Jesus).

> "a high-altitude explosion of color, sound, entertainment, and religious ceremony"

When You Go:

Copacabana is very pretty and friendly. It's usually cold, but take lots of sunscreen and a hat anyway because even on overcast days you can burn due to the altitude. While there, check out the tortora boats made of long bundles of reeds, and make an excursion to Isla Kalahuta, which is known for its stone tombs. Legend has it that these led to an underground Incan network of passageways which went all the way to Cuzco, Peru, the Inca capital.

Web Coordinate:

www.whatsgoingon.com/100things/candelaria

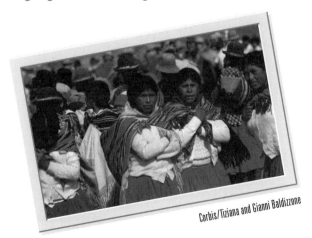

Corbis/Tiziana and Gianni Baldizzone

Carnaval

Sambodrome and Various Locations, Rio de Janeiro, Brazil

GPS Lat: 22.88333 S Lon: 043.28333 W

The great equalizer of Rio de Janeiro is its Carnaval celebration. For four days and nights, the country stops doing everything else and focuses on having one of the wildest and sexiest parties in the world. Adding to the locals, an estimated 300,000 foreign visitors cram into Rio for the hoopla! You have to see

Annual, January/ February

(four days before Ash Wednesday)

it to believe it—especially the two-day musical and dancing marathon that's organized by Rio's best samba associations.

Brazilians spend all year planning for Carnaval. Even the most impoverished save to buy costumes, often elaborate embroidered masterpieces. Preparation and pre-party parties are almost as much fun as the celebration itself. During Carnaval, plan to see at least one street band (banda), attend at least one ball, and spend plenty of time at the Sambodrome (samba central).

Carnaval's celebratory atmosphere is contagious and inspiring—everyone from children to grandparents lets loose for a few days. Barely there costumes and suggestive dancing infuse the celebrations. Although complete public nudity is against the law, a few strategically placed Band-Aids can do the trick.

Unexpectedly, Carnaval's main event doesn't happen on the streets of Rio anymore. Main festivities stay within the walls of the government-owned Sambodrome. Rental of a prime mezzanine box can cost tens of thousands of dollars! Bleacher seats are much more affordable, but really poor folk watch the twenty hours of action from atop crowded bridges and rooftops around the massive Sambodrome. Samba processions feature scantily clad samba dancers and national celebrities riding atop fabulously ornate floats.

Outside the stadium, Carnaval balls range from luxurious to licentious. Hundreds of them happen at clubs and halls all over Rio, and tickets are surprisingly cheap. Most are open to the public but, as expected, the exclusive balls can be the most exciting. Schmooze with stars at the exclusive Gala Ball, or experience the more outrageous, sexual side of Carnaval at less exclusive singles balls and gay balls. Put on your skimpiest costume to set the mood, and prepare yourself for an evening of throbbing salsa.

> "one of the wildest and sexiest parties in the world"

No one can resist the passion of Carnaval—its vivacious spirit permeates the city, infecting visitors and natives alike. This is your chance to experience one of the world's best parties while getting to know the very sensual, warm people of Brazil.

When You Go:

Plan for comfort: take some earplugs to wear at deafening balls and a foam cushion to pad your butt in the Sambodrome. In the Sambodrome, sit in Sections 5, 7, 9, or 11 for the best view. With 600 neighborhood block parties, you'll be hard-pressed to choose one or two, so make friends with someone who can suggest one (it's not hard to make friends with Brazilians). But don't wander into the seedier sections of the city, such as the area a few blocks behind Copacabana Beach, which can be dangerous.

Web Coordinate :

www.whatsgoingon.com/100things/riocarnaval

Copyright Don Klein

Reveillon Rio

Rio de Janeiro, Brazil

GPS Lat: 22.88333 S Lon: 043.28333 W

When New Year's rolls around, take a trip to Rio de Janeiro, the city of beaches, sensuality, and locals whose walks swing like a samba. Brazil's second biggest party of the year is Reveillon Rio, a New Year's celebration that combines the sea, spirituality, and a riotous party to set the year off right.

Annual, December 31

Millions of locals and visitors carouse on Copacabana and Ipanema Beaches, hobnob at hotel parties, and caper in clubs around Rio de Janeiro on New Year's Eve, proving that when Brazilians throw a party, they really throw a party. That funky fusion of African, Christian, and native traditions and characteristic Brazilian friendliness are what make Rio *the* place to forget the past and focus on the future.

You might want to hit the hotels and clubs to begin the revelry, but first head for the center of Rio life—the beach. Rio's Copacabana Beach is home to the most unique rite of Reveillon, when locals mix up spirituality and indulgence as only they know how. An estimated one million people gather on the beach to pay their respects to Iemanja, the goddess of the sea. In her honor, everyone dresses in white and carries *macumbas*, or offerings, to the sea. These tiny candlelit boats are scattered along the water's edge, waiting to be taken out to sea. All along the beach, with music emanating from large speakers, people pray and dance until sunrise.

According to Reveillon tradition, on New Year's Eve Brazilians must jump three waves, make some sort of prayer or wish, and throw flowers into the sea. Locals are so charming that they'll have you rolling up your white pants and jumping in the sea, but first make sure you're wearing the right undies to show through that wet white fabric. By Rio tradition, the color of underwear you wear at Reveillon expresses a wish that you have for love in the new year.

"a New Year's celebration that combines the sea, spirituality, and a riotous party"

When you're all wet, there's no place else to go but crazy. So down a *caipirinha*, a strong Brazilian drink made of sugar-cane alcohol, sugar, limes, and ice. Then wander around, listen to the live entertainment, and make friends with the locals (who will undoubtedly share their wine, food, and good cheer) until midnight, when the sky lights up with wild fireworks displays all along the beach.

When You Go:

There are lots of hotels, but they fill up fast for this celebration, so make plans in advance. Wear a money belt to safeguard against pickpockets who prey on drunken tourists. Forget about doing anything on January 1. Everyone sleeps in and many shops are closed because of an epidemic of hangovers.

Web Coordinate :

www.whatsgoingon.com/100things/reveillon

Copyright Don Klein

Día de Los Muertos (Day of the Dead)

Puebla, Mexico

GPS Lat: 19.05000 N Lon: 098.16666 W

Imagine honoring deceased loved ones by eating candy skulls inscribed with their names, dancing in skeleton costumes, and partying at their gravesides! That's how families in Mexico celebrate el Día de Los Muertos, or the Day of the Dead, an unusual celebration where the line between life and death is erased.

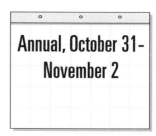

Annual, October 31– November 2

From October 31 to November 2 Mexicans party, pray, eat, and drink with visiting spirits of their dead friends and relatives. Particularly exuberant celebrations take place in Oaxaca, in southern Mexico, and Puebla, a large city southeast of Mexico City. Oaxaca is a beautiful colonial town, but Puebla's celebration of Día de Los Muertos is less overrun by tourists.

The Day of the Dead mixes ancient culture with new, bringing the Aztec notions of death, which represented a journey, to a Catholic culture that normally fears death. Aztecs considered life to be a dream and death the awakening.

Today, the Day of the Dead is a modernized version of the two-month Aztec celebration of death and reunion with the dead. It begins on October 31, when children parade around the streets dressed in Halloween-like costumes, and families build altars to decorate with food, hot chocolate, and toys for *angelitos*, or the spirits of departed children. Overnight, the angelitos arrive and remove the essence of the gifts, and in the morning, living children enjoy the real toys.

On November 1 (All Saints' Day), angelitos leave and families await the spirits of dead adults, filling altars with their favorite foods, tequila, and presents. Days are spent at home, "visiting" with the dead. Street vendors offer the opportunity to buy sugar skulls inked with the names of dead loved ones. Folk art is decorated with skeletons and skulls—everything from little figures to skull necklaces.

During the nights, altars adorned with photographs, flowers, and food are taken to the graves of the deceased. Families and friends hold vigils, dance, sing, pray . . . and drink lots of mescal! Salsa musicians roam the streets dressed as corpses, drummers travel the streets in ghoulish costumes, and dancers perform devil dances to ward off evil.

Spend a few days in a place where, for a time, death and life are linked together. Prowl the graveyards of Puebla to indulge your inner mortician—here, it's not considered spooky, weird, or morbid. Indeed, it's sure to be life-affirming, spirit-lifting, and certainly good for your soul!

> "an unusual celebration where the line between life and death is erased"

When You Go:

Puebla's in the shadows and ashes of feisty and very active volcano Popocatepetl (known affectionately as "El Popo")—so it's a good idea to check up on its activity before your journey. Take some photos of deceased loved ones and a few bucks to buy the proper folk art for your altar. Remember not to drink the water, but don't be surprised if you get sick anyway. Just keep the Immodium nearby.

Web Coordinate

www.whatsgoingon.com/100things/muertos

The Mexico Ministry of Tourism

Monarch Butterfly Migration

Angangueo, Michoacan, Mexico

GPS Lat: 19.20000 N Lon: 100.16666 W

What's the most beautiful insect? The jury's out, but the whimsical monarch butterfly is a very serious contender for that title. Now, imagine so many monarch butterflies flying above you that they form an orange and black cloud, or so many perched on trees that they look like thick clusters of leaves

Annual, December through mid-March

and you can't see the trees underneath. This fantasy is the reality at the most beautiful insect invasion in the world, the annual migration of the monarch butterflies.

Many people are unaware that, like birds, many butterfly species head south for the winter. In the early autumn across the USA and Canada one can find monarch butterflies gathering in preparation to make their journeys south. These little hustlers gather mostly on evergreen trees in places where there are abundant supplies of strength-giving nectar. In September they begin their migration to Mexico, often traveling over 2,000 miles!

The butterflies, the *Danaus plexippus* species, head for a few choice spots in Mexico for their winter vacation, since they can't survive the cold northern weather. But they can't survive in hot sunlight, either, so they find their way to the constant temperature and deep shade of the oyamel fir trees in the forests over three hours west of Mexico City, in the south-central state of Michoacan. From 100 to 250 million monarch butterflies show up throughout November and can be seen until mid-March in this high-altitude area, about 10,000 feet above sea level.

The butterflies have been making this migration for the last 40,000 years. In recent years, however, there has been a threat to the survival of the butterflies, due to logging and development. But the Mexican government and conservation groups are stepping in, and

many wintering areas are now protected (nine of about fourteen sites). Four of these are near the mountain village of Angangueo, north of the city of Zitácuaro. Here, the weather, trees, streams, and heavy fog are ideal for the monarchs. They cover every tree, and the whole area is flooded with orange!

In mid-March, the butterflies head back north to lay their eggs. During the spring and summer, two or three more generations are born, each flying progressively farther north, until they all turn around and fly back to Mexico in the fall. The butterflies showing up in Mexico include the great-great-grandchildren of those that left the previous spring. Monarchs live about two years, so the butterflies, lucky them, visit Mexico twice in their lives.

When You Go:

Zitácuaro is about three hours west of Mexico City or two hours east of Morelia, and Angangueo is forty-five minutes north of Zitácuaro. The best time to visit is February or early March. Pick a day with clear skies and warm sun. If the butterflies warm up enough, they'll flutter around from tree to tree, and you'll be able to hear their beating wings and have a better look at their flaming orange color.

"the most beautiful insect invasion in the world"

Web Coordinate:

www.whatsgoingon.com/100things/monarch

Vernal Equinox at Chichen Itza

Temple of Kukulkan, Chichen Itza, Yucatan, Mexico

GPS Lat: 20.83333 N Lon: 089.00000 W

On the first day of spring, Mother Earth, Father Sun, and Sister Moon are having a party. A couple of gods, a mystic constellation, and a big serpent are coming, and you're invited too! Welcome to the celebration of the Vernal Equinox at Chichen Itza in the Yucatan Peninsula of Mexico, an amazing astronomical occurrence at the spiritual center of the Earth on the first day of spring each year.

Annual, March 20

Chichen Itza was a Mayan center, the home of one of the most advanced of the American cultures back fifty or so generations. Why is the Vernal (or Spring) Equinox a big deal at Chichen Itza? Because the pyramid of Kulkulkan there is at the exact center of the four seasons. The pyramid has ninety-one steps on each of its four sides, representing the ninety-one days in each season. On March 20, when the sun passes directly overhead, it makes shadows in exact 90-degree angles on each of the four sides of the pyramid. At this time, the shadow of a wild serpent known as Quetzalcoatl emerges on part of the pyramid.

The celebration of the Vernal Equinox at Chichen Itza is a big deal for three reasons. One, you can appreciate the visual treat of watching Quetzalcoatl wend its way up the side of the pyramid, a result of a marvel of astrology and advanced pyramid engineering (this is the only day of the year when the sun's angle enables you to see this shadow). Two, you can choose to learn more about the fascinating Mayan culture by seeking the knowledge encrypted in the sacred Mayan calendars, perhaps with the use of sacred plants and through meditation (thereby uniting and harmonizing yourself with the Earth). And three, you can join the huge 60,000-person party of strangers at the pyramid!

The Mexico Ministry of Tourism

The visual and engineering aspects of this event are easy to grasp—it took incredible math and construction expertise to build this pyramid in just the right way. The spiritual side may be a bit harder to understand—the Mayans believed that the seven centers of our physical bodies connect at this time with the Pleiades star cluster, the "seven sisters" part of the Taurus constellation. Perhaps easiest to grasp, however, is the tequila. Enjoy the party!

When You Go:

Chichen Itza is in the middle of a Mayan cultural area. But one of the best things about a trip to Chichen Itza is that it's halfway between the towns of Cancun and Merida, about 100 miles from each. Thus, on your trip to soak up Mayan culture you can also have fun in the sun at Cancun party central and enjoy a taste of colonial Mexico in charming Merida.

"an amazing astronomical occurrence at the spiritual center of the Earth"

Web Coordinate:

www.whatsgoingon.com/100things/chichen

Semana Santa

Ayacucho, Peru

GPS Lat: 13.15000 S Lon: 074.21666 W

If you think painting a couple of boiled eggs and sitting in on Midnight Mass is a fun Easter activity, you haven't been to Peru during Semana Santa, where the mass commission of sins is expected! Peru's the place for one of the most pious and bizarre celebrations of Holy Week in the world.

Annual, March/April
(week before Easter Sunday)

Imagine yourself prostrate, averting your eyes from the statue of the Lord of the Earthquakes. You're looking away because if you don't, Jesus might choose you to die this year. You're praying to Christ to spare your city from the devastation of earthquakes. But if it's not done just right—including special underwear and a wig for the statue—the city might be destroyed.

That's just an example of the kind of extravagant ceremony you'll witness in the southern city of Ayacucho during Semana Santa. Each day is filled with displays of religious devotion—effigies, processions, and prostration galore. Peruvians have a history of being fervent about their religion, incorporating object worship, fear, and self-denial. Like the Greeks, Incans spent much time appeasing their many gods. Add Christiantity to paganistic frenzy and what do you expect? The combination makes a scene of ardent idol-worshipping celebration that would have made Moses weep.

Good Friday's procession of the holy sepulchre, recreating Christ in his tomb, is the most spectacular display of the week. In the Santo Domingo Church, a line of eager worshipers passes by an effigy of Jesus, wiping the Lord's wounds in a demonstration of devotion. Then, the coffin is carried away. With the entire city's lights extinguished, all attention is turned to the light emanating from the glass case carried high above the heads of the pallbearers. Attendants dressed in black and carrying thousands of burning candles follow the holy coffin, while musicians play a heart-wrenching melody.

Peruvians don't waste time getting over the death of their Lord (he'll be back). A popular belief is that since Christ is dead during the short period before the resurrection, he cannot be offended by anything on Earth. So on Friday and Saturday, Peruvians have license to behave however they like without divine repercussions. There is always a rash of wanton sex, robbery, and cheating, as well as many other licentious acts among the citizens at this time. No use in wasting the opportunity, right?

Corbis/Brian Vikander

When You Go:

Ayacucho is southeast of a big Peruvian city, Cuzco. Cuzco's relatively safe, but be careful elsewhere. A cab will take you the short ride from Cuzco into Ayacucho, where you won't need a car, since the city is easily traversed on foot. Travel and board are relatively inexpensive in Peru, but if you run out of cash, you can always wait until Friday and Saturday, when it will be okay to steal whatever you want to eat.

Web Coordinate:

www.whatsgoingon.com/100things/semanasanta

> "one of the most pious and bizarre celebrations of Holy Week in the world"

Los Diablos Danzantes
(Devil Dancers of Corpus Christi)

Los Caneyes, Patanemo, Venezuela

GPS Lat: 10.48333 N Lon: 068.03333 W

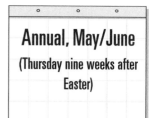

Annual, May/June
(Thursday nine weeks after Easter)

Have you never danced with the devil? Well, here's your chance. During Corpus Christi in the Venezuelan village of Los Caneyes, you can get down with Beelzebub and his buddies in a passionate celebration melding Afro-Caribbean traditions with Roman Catholic beliefs. The ornery fiends do a little jig from house to house in observance of Corpus Christi, a celebration in honor of the Eucharist.

The "*hermanos*," or brothers, who participate in the devilish dancing don elaborate red costumes with horned and streamered masks and bells on their feet. Each year, hermanos spend the day dancing, banging drums, and shaking maracas. They are bound by a pledge to dance for eight consecutive years. They made the pledge in exchange for an exceptional plea to God for divine intervention—to cure an illness for example.

For the confraternities of devil-dancing hermanos, cutting a rug is serious business. According to their strong faith, if they fail to fulfill the holy promise, they will be punished severely by God. The dancing is rigorous, serving to exorcise evil influences from the village and to restore harmony. Hermanos dance their way down the "old road" to the village church. When the devils arrive at the church, the entire town participates in a maypole dance.

Next, the devils gather at an altar in front of the church. Two by two, they dance and leap toward the church and prostrate themselves, rendering homage to Jesus Christ, their "Overlord." Then the devil dancers, representing evil, try to sneak into the church. They form a human cross to trick the church into thinking they're reverent. They ascend the church steps several times but are pushed back by church officials.

Repelled from the church, devil dancers visit each house in town, dancing and beating their drums. They visit the homes to drive the devils and evil out of them. The dancers writhe to the beat of the drums, intimidating and frightening the citizens of the village, who must obey the dancers' demands of gifts of soup and other items. Special attention is paid to the houses of the recently deceased.

> "a passionate celebration melding Afro-Caribbean traditions with Roman Catholic beliefs"

When it comes time for a little spring cleansing, take a trip to Venezuela to have your devils removed by the hermanos most qualified for the job!

When You Go:

Los Caneyes lies a couple of hours to the west of Caracas on the Caribbean Coast and is pretty remote. Venezuelan buses are air-conditioned and comfy—a much more comfortable alternative to trying to drive the country's treacherous roads. Get into your adventure mode: the little village of Los Caneyes does have at least one inn and restaurant, but it's not luxurious. In case you don't make it to Los Caneyes, devil dancing on Corpus Christi happens in locations throughout Venezuela.

Web Coordinate:

www.whatsgoingon.com/100things/devildancers

Juan Silva

Junkanoo

Nassau, Bahamas

GPS Lat: 25.05000 N Lon: 077.48333 W

If you're like many, you usually spend the days after Christmas and New Year's Eve in a funk: you're faced with the realization that you're not getting any more presents, you're bloated, and you have a hangover. Where better to go than the Bahamas, where the party is just getting started? Junkanoo is an ostentatious and exuberant Afro-Bahamian mega-party that gives you an excuse to ditch the sweaters and fruitcakes and head for warmer climes.

**Annual,
December 26 and
January 1**

From 2 A.M. to dawn on December 26 and again on January 1, the huge Junkanoo parade invades the streets of Nassau, beginning on Bay Street and circling downtown twice. Thousands of locals and tourists crowd the streets to gawk at the elaborately costumed "rushers" dancing down the street to jungle drums, cowbells, whistles, horns, and countless improvised instruments such as bicycle horns, wheel rims, and whistles.

The celebration of Junkanoo began during plantation times in the Caribbean Islands. Some slaves were given three days off at Christmas to see family and friends. Today, all communities of the Bahamas take part in Junkanoo, and it's highly promoted as a tourist attraction. Dances range from merengue to "short-step," a dance based on two steps forward and one step back, which is thought to have come from the African Ashanti warriors' march to war. The music is reminiscent of African traditional music, highly influenced by tribal instruments and rhythms.

Junkanoo is lots of fun to watch, but for local community troupes of "rushers" it's a charged competition. Judges award thousands of dollars in prize money to the best troupe on the day after the parade. For weeks before the parade, rushers sequester themselves in top-secret "Junkanoo shacks," preparing painfully intricate costumes, creative music, and dance routines, all based on a theme that is kept secret from other troupes—anything from an historic to futuristic motif.

Participants spend over twelve hours a day the week before Junkanoo creating detailed, colorful, full-body costumes from cardboard, glitter, sequins, and crepe paper. By the end of the parade the costumes are usually destroyed, but the best ones are restored to be displayed at the Junkanoo Expo museum.

> "an ostentatious and exuberant Afro-Bahamian mega-party"

So, pack your bags and head for Nassau for something that'll take your mind off of wilting Christmas trees and repeated radio renditions of "Auld Lang Syne."

When You Go:

If leisure's your thing, take a cruise that docks in the port of Nassau in time for Junkanoo. But if you hate flocks of tourists, stay away from the docks when the boats arrive to avoid the massive groups that invade Nassau's shops and restaurants. On the night of Junkanoo, stake out a good spot on Bay Street before the crowds take over. Don't forget your sunblock for the beach and a sweater in case it's chilly at night.

Web Coordinate:

www.whatsgoingon.com/100things/junkanoo

Bahamas Tourist Office

Saut d'Eau Vodou Pilgrimage

Saut d'Eau, Haiti

GPS Lat: 18.66666 N Lon: 072.33333 W

There's an old saying in Haiti that the country is 90 percent Catholic and 100 percent Vodou. For this impoverished nation, more than being Haiti's main religion, Vodou is a way of life. Back in the slavery days, Vodou survived under the guise of Catholicism. Today, this still makes for a fascinating mix. On July 15

**Annual,
July 15-16**

and 16 each year in the region of Saut d'Eau, there is a huge celebration that simultaneously honors the Virgin Mary and Erzulie, the Vodou Goddess of Love. If you go, you can pray at a church then participate in a real Vodou experience.

Vodou ceremonies involve powerful spirits, called *loa*, in rites that help determine the direction of people's lives. Such guidance is akin to the influence of Christian saints. Over the years, loa Erzulie, the Goddess of Love and Beauty (a cleansing, strong, and well-liked presence), became associated with the Virgin Mary.

On July 16, 1884, there was a reported appearance of the Virgin Mary in the charming village of Ville-Bonheur, in the area of Saut d'Eau. Every anniversary, pilgrims celebrate the apparition at the church built on that spot. They spend the night in front of the church, illuminated by thousands of candles. During the day, hundreds of women dressed in white climb a hill to a shrine of the Virgin, carrying rocks in their hands or on their heads to deposit with the Virgin. This gesture is meant to attract blessings, resolve problems, or even bring a curse to an enemy.

During these two days at Saut d'Eau, Vodou coexists very naturally with Christianity. Among the pilgrims to the Virgin are thousands of Vodou practitioners who trek over 2 miles to the Saut d'Eau waterfall, an oasis of freshness that is the home of loa Erzulie. The waterfall descends over 100 feet, among vines, shallow pools, and mossy ledges. Hundreds of Vodouists strip and bathe nude under the waterfall to purify themselves, and many shake and cry when they become possessed by Erzulie.

One thing that makes the Saut d'Eau rites so special is that the biggest Vodou personalities and most loyal devotees in Haiti congregate there for these two days. This fosters a carnival-like atmosphere with many Vodou camps. All around, people consult with *houngan* priests, Vodou drums beat incessantly, and sacrifices of chickens and oxen are made to Erzulie.

"a huge celebration that simultaneously honors the Virgin Mary and Erzulie, the Vodou Goddess of Love"

With its mixture of the Virgin, the Goddess of Love, and earthly influences, Saut d'Eau is a bazaar of blessed celebration and sensory overload. As they say in Haitian Creole, "*Bondye Bon*," or God is good!

When You Go:

Be careful—Haiti can be dangerous. Hiring a guide is helpful and can make your trip safer. Ville-Bonheur is two and a half hours northeast of Port-au-Prince, near the town of Mirebalais. This event is for hardened travelers, not tourists. Saut d'Eau is rural Haiti, and modern conveniences don't exist. Take a tent, or you can rent a room in the home of a local family for very little money. In either case, you may have to visit the great outdoors when nature calls, so pack some toilet paper!

Web Coordinate:

www.whatsgoingon.com/100things/vodou

Associated Press/Daniel Morel

Europe

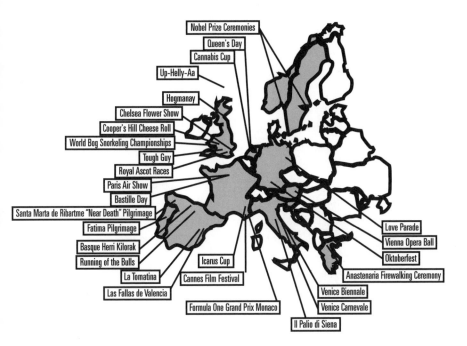

Nobel Prize Ceremonies
Queen's Day
Cannabis Cup
Up-Helly-Aa
Hogmanay
Chelsea Flower Show
Cooper's Hill Cheese Roll
World Bog Snorkeling Championships
Tough Guy
Royal Ascot Races
Paris Air Show
Bastille Day
Santa Marta de Ribartme "Near Death" Pilgrimage
Fatima Pilgrimage
Basque Herri Kilorak
Running of the Bulls
Icarus Cup
La Tomatina
Cannes Film Festival
Las Fallas de Valencia
Formula One Grand Prix Monaco
Il Palio di Siena
Venice Carnevale
Venice Biennale
Anastenaria Firewalking Ceremony
Oktoberfest
Vienna Opera Ball
Love Parade

Vienna Opera Ball

Staatsoper, Vienna, Austria

GPS Lat: 48.21666 N Lon: 016.36666 E

In Vienna, the word "ball" doesn't imply princes and pumpkins at midnight. There, balls are regular affairs, and the biggest of them all is the Vienna Opera Ball—where propriety is still in fashion, ball gowns are huge, and everyone knows how to dance the waltz. Head for the oldest and grandest ball in the world.

**Annual,
January/February**
(the week before Lent)

All guests make a big entrance at the Vienna Opera Ball, arriving at the front door not only in cars and taxis, but even in horse-drawn carriages. Ladies emerge from the vehicles wearing voluminous, flowing gowns and escorted by dapper gentlemen in the requisite coat and tails. Prominent artists and politicians join less-known folk (up to 7,000 of them) to waltz, drink champagne, and schmooze. The big entrance of the President of Austria signals the beginning of the night's festivities.

As the orchestra plays the evening's first polonaise, 200 debutante couples take the floor for the first waltz of the evening. Nervous young women dressed in long white gowns and tiny crowns are swept around the floor by nervous young men. They spend months in classes preparing for this big debut, as the Viennese waltz is the hardest of all waltzes, involving sweeping turns and difficult footwork.

Once it begins, the music doesn't stop until five o'clock the next morning. And although Strauss and friends traditionally get top billing, rooms around the State Opera House are set up with live bands playing popular music tailored for every age. For the less footloose, gambling is even available in the Opera Ball Casino.

The Vienna Opera Ball has thrived since 1935. It's the inspiration for over 300 balls offered every year in Vienna during ball season, from New Year's Eve until Ash Wednesday. Balls such as the Choco-

Austrian National Tourist Office, Inc.

late Ball are less formal, while the lawyers' and physicians' balls are elite. Despite the high cost of attending some balls, Viennese of all social classes usually go to at least one during the season.

The Opera Ball is one of the most expensive of Vienna's balls. Guests must purchase a seat at a table to have somewhere to sit between dances. Hosting a box is a major investment, and a glass of champagne can cost $30! But this is the ball not to miss, whether you're living it up in the President's box or propped up in the corner without anything to drink.

When You Go:

Don't drag your formal wear on the plane; rent a gown or tails from a local Viennese dress shop. To properly learn the Viennese waltz you would ideally spend a few months taking a class, but if you need to learn it in a jiffy, enroll in a class for tourists at a dance school in Vienna. Call the Opera Ball Office for tickets. Don't worry if advance planning is not your forte; several Vienna travel agencies specialize in gala balls.

> "the oldest and grandest ball in the world"

Web Coordinate:

www.whatsgoingon.com/100things/operaball

Chelsea Flower Show

Grounds of the Royal Hospital, London, England

GPS Lat: 51.50000 N Lon: 000.16666 W

Annual, May

Ever been to a flower show? Ever even considered going to a flower show? The annual Chelsea Flower Show in London, England, might interest even the most jaded souls.

Since its inception in 1913, the Chelsea Flower Show has evolved into the most prestigious horticulture show on the planet. Organized by the Royal Horticultural Society, the absolutely fabulous four-day show signals the unofficial start of the English summer social season. The floral extravaganza attracts 170,000 British and international visitors, who come to gawk at the buds, bouquets, and each other.

The action takes place on the 11-acre grounds of Sir Christopher Wren's Royal Hospital in Chelsea. The central focus is the Grand Marquee, a 3.5 acre tent that weighs over 65 tons (it's noted in the *Guinness Book of World Records* as the world's largest tent). Under and around the Marquee, over 700 exhibitors display a variety of flora, from grand floral arrangements to full-scale landscaped gardens.

The indisputable highlight is the fantasy show gardens. These opulent, expensive displays take on many unique themes, from a recreation of the Prince of Wales's organic gardens at Highgrove House to an interpretation of Beatrix Potter's "Mr. McGregor's Garden" where Peter Rabbit lived. Celebrities and luminaries often add their talents to these extravagant creations. Personalities like fan-waving couturier Karl Lagerfeld, designer and restaurateur Sir Terrance Conran, and His Highness Sheikh Zayed bin Sultan Al Nahyan have shown their green thumbs in recent years.

Flowers aside, people-watching is probably the most entertaining feature of the event. Everyone dresses up for the occasion, and many of the women in attendance wear outrageous hats. During the show these thirsty fashion plates down over 6,000 bottles of champagne and 300,000 cups of tea.

Not a single clipping or bud goes on sale until the final day (always on Friday), when a bell is rung at 4:30 P.M. to signal the end of the show. The scene immediately turns into a madhouse as every wannabe gardener eagerly pulls out some pounds in an attempt to take home a piece of the show. At least one little old lady has been known to get out of her wheelchair and use it as a shopping cart, and chic Sloane Ranger yuppies have been known to buy up entire show gardens to take out to their country homes.

> "the most prestigious horticulture show on the planet"

When You Go:

Tickets need to be booked well in advance for the Thursday and Friday public viewings (the show sells out every year). The first two days of the show (always Tuesday and Wednesday) are open exclusively to members of the Royal Horticultural Society. You might consider joining the RHS; besides the privileged viewings at the show, you'll receive complimentary admittance to 271 of the U.K.'s most beautiful gardens, a monthly magazine, free seeds, and free gardening advice.

Web Coordinate:

www.whatsgoingon.com/100things/flowershow

Britain on View/Stockwave

Cooper's Hill Cheese Roll

Cooper's Hill, Brockworth, Gloucestershire, England

GPS Lat: 51.78333 N Lon: 002.25000 W

Once a year, the tiny town of Brockworth, England, gets very excited about
chasing cheeses down a steep hill. They
call it the Cooper's Hill Cheese Roll, an
out-of-control, gravity-defying contest,
and they've been doing it for 200 years
as a spring fertility rite. The cheesy
chase draws thousands of spectators to

Annual, May

(last Monday, Spring Bank
Holiday)

the hillside. Everyone from the mayor to local boys and girls has pursued the great wheel of Double Gloucester down the 1,000-foot
descent.

To begin the Cooper's Hill Cheese Roll, the vicar of Cooper's Hill
stands at the top of the slope, declaring, "One to be ready, two to be
steady, three to be prepared, and four away!" Then he sends the
cheese whirling down the hill, pursued by a boisterous mob of cheese
chasers. In four different races open to all comers (one is ladies only),
the bold, mostly boozed-up crazies scramble down the hill in an effort
to catch the cheese.

Cheese Roll committee member Tony Peasley explains that the
cheese run isn't necessarily a run. "It's a steep hill," he says. "The
angle of the slope is around 60 degrees. . . . Imagine a person trying
to run down a hill that steep. The sheer physics of the situation won't
allow them to stay on their feet. They'll be bouncing, with their arms
and legs going everywhere." Indeed, most racers tumble, bounce,
and roll down the hill after the runaway cheese, which can get going
as fast as 32 mph—way faster than a human can run.

Since most people don't stay on their feet during the run, injuries
are unavoidable. Peasley explains, "There is an element of risk
involved. We've had the occasional dislocation, but we haven't
(touch wood) had many serious injuries. This is part of the fun of the
whole thing." During one year's roll, twenty-four competitors, seven

crowd members, and two ambulance men sustained everything from minor sprains to broken arms. A spectator suffered head injuries when, trying to avoid a runaway cheese, he lost his balance and fell 100 feet down the hillside.

The Citizen, Gloucester, U.K.

The reward for all this carnage? Winners get to keep the flat rounds of Double Gloucester cheese used during the races. Local cheese maker Diana Smart specially forms each round to weigh about 7.5 pounds and measure 10 inches in diameter. "If it were bigger, it could get quite dangerous," she suggests. It's a good thing it's not any more dangerous!

When You Go:

Get yourself to Gloucester, and then it's not far to Cooper's Hill. Brockworth is a tiny (and not tourist-oriented) town, so plan to stay in nearby Cheltenham. If you'll be chasing the cheese, pack some painkillers and knee pads and make friends with the St. John's Ambulance team. Should you win the cheese, beware of British Customs—they don't like anyone to leave the country with dairy products.

> "an out-of-control, gravity-defying contest"

Web Coordinate:

www.whatsgoingon.com/100things/cheeseroll

Royal Ascot Races

Ascot Raceway, Berkshire, England

GPS Lat: 51.51666 N Lon: 001.33333 W

You may not like formality or rules, but you're a rare person indeed if you're not interested in the ways of the British upper crust. The Royal Ascot Races, almost 300 years old, are meant to be about horses, but what they're really about is people-watching. The tone is set at 2 P.M. each day, before the cup races

Annual, June

begin, when the Queen herself travels around the racecourse in a carriage. The entire royal family, and all the hangers-on, will turn out at some point during this competition, the most pompous of horse races.

In pure British style, the racecourse seating area is divided into several "classes." The elite Royal Enclosure is restricted mostly to Brits who have attended before or been sponsored by prior attendees. Americans can apply to the American Embassy in London, which is allocated several hundred tickets for the former colonists. Alternatively, the Grandstand Enclosure is easier to get into, but still a little snooty. The Silver Ring seating is where the proletariat plops down.

While the dress code isn't too strict in the Grandstand Enclosure, and there's no dress code in the Silver Ring, the Royal Enclosure has rigid rules. (Think Audrey Hepburn in *My Fair Lady*, which featured these races.) Ladies must wear "formal day dress with a hat that covers the crown of the head." Men must wear top hats and morning coats. Outfits appearing at this high-society "English Season" event, particularly on "Ladies Day" Thursday, will be seen in the British tabloids for weeks to come!

There are twenty-four races over four days, and over £2 million in prize money. Highlights include the St. James's Palace Stakes on Tuesday, the top European mile race for three-year-old colts and geldings. The Coronation Stakes race on Wednesday is the fillies' equivalent. Thursday's highlights include the Gold Cup, one of the longest flat races in the world (2.5 miles) and the top race for stayers, and the King Edward VII Stakes. Friday's King's Stand Stakes is also a prime race.

There's lots of gawking and lots of serious racing. But this is not some reserved day in the park. The nearly 250,000 attendees down 50,000 bottles of champagne, 2.5 tons of beef, 2.25 tons of fresh salmon, and 4,500 lobsters! Enjoy yourself, but just make sure you don't get carried away, like Audrey Hepburn's Liza Doolittle, who yelled, "Come on Dover! Move your bloomin' arse!" at a racehorse. That would draw looks.

"the most pompous of horse races"

When You Go:

Put on your formal wear, even if you won't be sitting in the Royal Enclosure; you'll fit in better, have a lot more fun, and maybe even make it into the papers. Make sure you have a ticket when you show up; no tickets are sold at the gate. Joan Collins was allegedly turned away one year for lack of one. And why not hire a limo for the trip? A Bentley will do just fine.

Web Coordinate:

www.whatsgoingon.com/100things/ascot

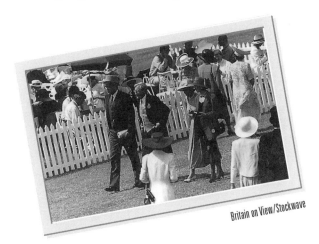

Britain on View/Stockwave

Tough Guy

Old Perton, South Staffordshire, England

GPS Lat: 52.88333 N Lon: 002.03333 W

So you think you're tough? Here's a race guaranteed to reduce you to a whimpering, shivering mess of a human. It's the roughest, most over-the-top extreme sports event ever. It's Tough Guy, a race whose obstacle course boasts three times the number of "punishing assault obstacles" as Marine training courses.

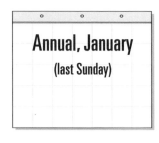

Annual, January
(last Sunday)

Tough Guy was started by ex-Grenadier Guard and military assault course builder Billy Wilson, known as "Mr. Mouse." Since it began in 1986, the event has raised hundreds of thousands of pounds for charity. About 4,000 "deliriously mad" competitors from the United Kingdom and Europe—including hundreds of women—show up every year for Tough Guy. Participants anywhere from age fifteen to age eighty-two set out on an 8-mile obstacle course, but the first competitor isn't expected to cross the finish line until over an hour and a half later—it's that hard.

Entrants must do a "warm-up" run of 8 miles before embarking on the fierce assault course, "The Killing Fields." Sloshing through acres of icy water, mud pits, and swamps, they are pushed to their limits with obstacles like Murder Mile, Fiery Holes, the Barbed Wire Crawl, and the Behemoth Tree-Top Rope Crossing.

The Viet Cong Saigon Blackhole Tunnels of Terror are particularly tough. Competitors crawl through small, muddy tunnels dug deep into the hillside. Climbing "The Tiger" is no romp through the tulips, either—it's a 30 by 150-foot monster laced with electric shock wires set at twice the strength of that used in deterring cattle! After all their tree climbing, jungle crawling, and mud-pit crossing, the freezing, miserable competitors must finally take the Underwater Swim through a murky 12-foot tunnel.

They emerge to join a chaotic scene of babbling, hugging, hot-tea drinking, and puking. Every finisher is wrapped in a foil thermal wrap. One year, of 3,600 competitors, there were at least 365 cases of serious hypothermia. Amazingly, no one has died at Tough Guy, though near-deaths and injuries abound. The hundreds of marshals (on-course guardians) and "Florence Nightingales" are kept very busy.

Even though the Tough Guy course is the earthly equivalent of Hell, every year people flock to join the race. Every year the waiting list grows. For many, the pure glory of having survived the nightmare of Tough Guy is enough. But for others, it's all about winning. Considering that the winner gets only a medal and a hot shower, though, surviving sounds just fine!

When You Go:

If you want to race, register way in advance and don't skimp on training! All competitors must go through pre-race training that includes crawling through thickets, slithering under a ground sheet with a paper bag on one's head, and stair diving. You'll get newsletters from the Tough Guy crew, with tips on race survival and training. When Tough Guy rolls around, pack extra energy bars and a lightweight water container, and then . . . pray.

> "the roughest, most over-the-top extreme sports event ever"

Web Coordinate:

www.whatsgoingon.com/100things/toughguy

Bastille Day (Fête Nationale)

Paris, France

GPS Lat: 48.86666 N Lon: 002.33333 E

Annual, July 14

There is nothing like Gallic pride, and there's nothing like Bastille Day. After all, this is the spirited independence day celebration of the Republic of France. The "official program" is surprisingly lean, but there are fabulous public and private parties in the streets, firehouses, nightclubs, discos, and parking garages all over Paris.

The date commemorates the beginning of the French Revolution, when angry commoners stormed the Bastille fortress to free the political prisoners incarcerated there. (Only seven prisoners were there at the time; that's something they don't tell you when you go to see *Les Miserables*.) This assault was the start of the fall of the stuffy, out-of-touch French monarchy and signaled the beginning of an intellectual movement that ultimately produced one of the most important proclamations in history—The Declaration of the Rights of Man and of the Citizen.

Start your adventure at the scene of the crime—the Place de la Bastille. The prison was demolished a couple of centuries ago, and now you'll find a hectic traffic circle and the towering Column de Bastille. But there is always a rowdy crowd there for the Fête Nationale.

The most unique "official" events are the *bals des pompiers*, or firemen's balls, which take place at nearly all the fire stations in the city. The schedule can be confusing—not all stations hold balls, and some hold them on July 12, some on July 13, a few on July 14, and some hold them all three nights. But one thing is certain: You'll find plenty of beer and dancing in the streets (probably with Parisian firefighters).

Other *bals* occur all over Paris during the days preceding the Fête Nationale. One of the most prestigious is the *Grand Bal*, usually held in the Tuileries Gardens.

Bastille Day begins with the traditional military parade down the Champs-Elysées. Reviewing stands are erected at the Place de la Concorde facing the Arc de Triomphe, and the parade starts at the Etoile and marches straight down the boulevard towards the Louvre.

French Government Tourist Office

Fête Nationale's finale is a fireworks display near the Eiffel Tower in the Champs de Mars. The "Pyro-Show" begins around 10 P.M., and, if the weather is good, over 100,000 people show up (this is the only day of the year when people are allowed on the Champs de Mars lawn). It's an explosive way to conclude this victorious day!

When You Go:

Face it, there are so many events and parties happening on Bastille Day that you'll never see everything. Pick up a newspaper for concert and event schedules and a round-up on the *bals de pompiers*. All you have to do, though, is listen for the music and follow the crowds. Or, if you are feeling lazy, you can watch the fanfare as the troops of the Foreign Legion march by on television.

> "the spirited independence day celebration of the Republic of France"

Web Coordinate:

www.whatsgoingon.com/100things/bastille

Cannes Film Festival

Cannes, France

GPS Lat: 43.55000 N Lon: 007.00000 W

The best place to mingle with celebrities and pretend you're famous is at the Cannes Film Festival, where you (and 250,000 other gawkers) can see hundreds of movie stars. While this spectacle may fuel dreams of your own fame and fortune, it can also be a reality check. You may imagine yourself sipping

Annual, May

Dom Perignon on the Hotel Carlton beach with stars in swimsuits, bikinis, or even topless. But instead you may spend your time pleading to get into a dumpy motel a half hour away, then eating at McDonald's because you can't get into any restaurants.

Regardless, you can't help but enjoy yourself at the festival. After all, this *is* paradise, the French Riviera! Over 30,000 film industry people attend the Cannes Film Festival to honor the year's best films. The nucleus is the juried "Palme d'Or" award, held in the Palais des Festival building. The screenings of the twenty-two chosen films are super-exclusive and by invitation only. But you may want to hang out anyway, since lots of star sightings happen outside the Palais on the main drag, La Croisette.

In addition to the Palme d'Or screenings, there are eight "Films Out of Competition" screened, plus four films competing for the "Camera d'Or" award. Other awards include the Grand Jury Prize, Best Director, Best Actress, and Best Actor. There are also special programs, such as "Cinefoundation" for student filmmakers and a "Tribute to Producers." Over 500 films are screened officially and unofficially during the twelve-day festival, so you can probably catch a few unofficial screenings around town.

The other purposes of the festival are promotion and deal making. The epicenter of Cannes networking is the Hotel Carlton, where all the big studio dogs gather. The lobby teems with actors, actresses,

Serge Carrie', Phototheque SEMEC Cannes

producers, directors, distributors, and writers meeting and doing interviews. And there are parties: huge parties, small parties, all night, all day. On boats, on barges, and on beaches. In hotels, poolside, and in rented private villas. You can crash some of these, but you've got to be very, very inventive.

Your vision of the Cannes Film Festival may have been shaped by the international starlets of days past, like Brigitte Bardot, Catherine Deneuve, Sophia Loren, and Ursula Andress, usually seen on the beach wearing Persol sunglasses and very little else. But now that Cannes is crawling with huge American stars, it is more like Hollywood-by-the-Sea than France. Maybe not quite as sophisticated as before, but just as glamorous and exciting!

When You Go:

One thousand films are usually submitted for consideration, but only a few are chosen for screening. The biggest stars stay in the Hotel du Cap Eden Roc, which is booked months in advance. Rooms cost around $1,000 a night. If you get burned out on the Cannes scene, head south about forty-five minutes to St. Tropez to sip a *pastis* on the waterfront, or head north about the same distance to Monte Carlo to gamble a little.

> "the best place to mingle with celebrities and pretend you're famous"

Web Coordinate:

www.whatsgoingon.com/100things/cannes

Icarus Cup Masquerade Flights (Coupe Icare)

Saint Hilaire du Touvet, France

GPS Lat: 45.18333 N Lon: 005.71666 E

Annual, September

If you want to jump off a 3,000-foot cliff while stuffed inside a cow, crucified on a cross, or jammed into a massive orange traffic cone, think again. It's been done. You'll have to think up something more original to win the 100,000 francs at stake in the Icarus Cup Masquerade Flights that are staged above St. Hilaire du Touvet, in the French Alps near Grenoble.

It's all a part of the Icarus Cup, four days of flying fun every September since 1974. About eighty zany paraglider and hang glider pilots participate by jumping off high cliffs dressed as, say, the Three Little Pigs, Laurel and Hardy in a car, or a large kangaroo. This is the funniest and most fun flying festival on Earth!

The most amusing place to watch the Masquerade Flights shenanigans is at the take-off area, the frightful cliff above the small village of St. Hilaire. Pilots struggle to get off the ground while wearing their complicated costumes, before struggling even more to land upright in the valley below! Most people view the antics from the village, where the vantage point is also good for watching aerial ballets, acrobatic shows, kites, gliders, hot air balloons, and more.

The Icarus Cup allows hang gliding, paragliding, ballooning, and other motorless and ultralight flight enthusiasts to gather each year for a multifaceted celebration of free flight, highlighted by the Masquerade Flights. The event attracts over 6,000 pilots and 50,000 spectators each year and is one of the largest and most respected events of its kind in the world.

The Icarus Cup festivities also include the International Film Festival of Free Flight, which is open to films directly related to the air, wind, and powerless or ultralight flight. The International Salon of

Aerial Sports trade show allows for wheeling and dealing with vendors of non-motorized aerial sports gear.

Rounding out the to-do list are visiting the Museum of Free Flight, joining the Competition of Paper Planes, and watching several serious hang gliding and paragliding competitions, such as the Spot Landing Contest or the Cross Country Contest.

If your dream is to fly in the Masquerade Flights, it's never too early to start planning for next year. All you have to do is become a certified expert pilot, break out the sewing machine and buzz saw, and start working on your wild costume!

> "the funniest and most fun flying festival on Earth"

When You Go:

When traveling to the Icarus Cup, if you sit on the left side of the bus from Grenoble to St. Hilaire du Touvet, you'll get great views down the mountain. In St. Hilaire, take a ride on the funicular railway, which goes through the most inclined tunnel in the world at an angle of almost 45 degrees. It goes from Montfort in the Gresivaudan Valley to St. Hilaire.

Web Coordinate:

www.whatsgoingon.com/100things/icarus

26th Icarus Cup

Paris Air Show

Le Bourget Exhibition Center, Paris, France

GPS Lat: 48.86666 N Lon: 002.33333 E

Since its simple beginnings in 1909, the Paris Air Show has grown into the most prestigious and important air show on the planet. What started as a showcase for a radical and untested new form of transportation has become a huge spectacle both on the ground and in the skies above Paris.

Odd-numbered years, June

Over the years, impressive aeronautic advancements like the Concorde, the European Airbus, and the Space Shuttle have all made their public debut at the show.

Nearly 300,000 people come to see (and test) the latest in aerospace technology from thousands of exhibitors from around the world. Everyone from private arms dealers to international playboys drops by to take a look at what's new, so you can be guaranteed some excellent people-watching. And don't worry, even if you are not shopping for your own private jet or missile launcher, there is still plenty to keep you entertained at the Paris Air Show.

The show takes place at the Le Bourget Exhibit Center and Airport, about 6 miles from Paris. This location was once the main airport for the City of Light and was the spot where Charles Lindbergh touched down at the end of the first non-stop flight from New York to Paris in 1927. Today, exhibition areas for the show now take up nearly one million square feet.

Exhibits of everything from space vehicles to anti-aircraft defense systems are displayed in five mammoth exhibit halls. There are also national pavilions, where individual countries display their latest civil and military technologies. But the highlight is the outdoor "static exhibit" area, where hundreds of planes and helicopters await your inspection.

French Government Tourist Office

Flanking the outdoor exhibition areas are the "reception chalets," where the bigwigs come to haggle deals and sign contracts in a more private setting. Aircraft manufacturers even take their customers on test flights to show off their goods in the air.

For those not planning on making a purchase, you can still get the feel of it all from the ground during the daily flight presentations. Every afternoon for four hours the top aircraft take to the skies over the Le Bourget to dazzle the public below. The presentation is visible from all areas of the show grounds.

When You Go:

The Paris Air Show is open to the public during the weekends (and to the trade from Monday through Friday). Tickets for the public can be purchased at the main gate. Le Bourget is easily reached by public transit from Paris on either the Metro or RER (Réseau Express Régional). "The Village" at the air show offers banking and currency exchange facilities, along with boutiques selling aeronautically inspired merchandise like watches and sunglasses.

> "the most prestigious and important air show on the planet"

Web Coordinate:

www.whatsgoingon.com/100things/airshow

Love Parade

Ku'damm, Berlin, Germany

GPS Lat: 52.53333 N Lon: 013.41666 E

If you're in Berlin during the annual Love Parade, you'll get a peek at the biggest flock of freaks you'll ever see in one place! Every year, in the name of love, Berlin plays host to the largest party of international youth in the world when over one million people crowd the Ku'damm, one of Berlin's busiest streets.

Annual, July
(second Saturday)

Climb the nearest tree, and you'll see a sea of the outrageous: people with hearts shaved into their spray-painted heads, piercings, tattoos, platform shoes, leather S & M outfits, spiked jewelry, and more of the unimaginable.

It's the raver's wildest dream come true as the million or more techno-lovers writhe together on the packed Ku'damm. When the street gets too full, you'll find people dancing on phone booths and port-a-potties, standing on top of shrubbery, and even pulsating to the music while hanging from major traffic lights.

The Love Parade began in 1988 before the Berlin techno scene had become mainstream. A popular local disk jockey, Doktor Motte, gathered his 150 techno-raver friends to celebrate his birthday. Blasting techno music from large speakers set up in a Volkswagen bus, he led his gyrating friends down the Ku'damm in a Pied Piper scene of raver madness. The next year, the Love Parade's attendance was 2,000, and it has been exponentially increasing every year, reaching an attendance of over one million techno-heads!

A few dozen disk jockey trucks blast their beats as loudly as possible as they slowly crawl through the packed parade route. It is so loud that nearby bridges vibrate! Half of the trucks begin at one end of the route and half at the other, and they all end up at the Victory Column in Berlin's central park, the Tiergarten. In the evening, everyone crams into Berlin's techno clubs.

How did Doktor Motte and the Love Parade team get permission to make such a mess out of Berlin? "We registered a protest march which was named 'Peace, Pleasure, and Pancake,'" said Motte. "I gave the following reasons for it: Peace stands for worldwide disarmament. Pleasure stands for music as a means of global communication. Pancake stands for a just distribution of food in the world. And that's what I stand for!" Other "political" themes have included "The Spirit Makes You Move," "Demonstrate (for) Love," and "Worldwide Partypeople Weekend."

> "the biggest flock of freaks you'll ever see in one place!"

When You Go:

The Berlin government asks parade-goers not to use the very efficient train station in the center of the city, so that the Berlin transport system does not collapse. Take a bus into the city and travel on the U-Bahn, the underground train system. Be warned: at the last minute, it's nearly impossible to find accommodations other than a little bit of grass in the park (and that only if you're lucky).

Web Coordinate:

www.whatsgoingon.com/100things/loveparade

Berlin Tourism's Marketing

Oktoberfest

Theresienwiese, Munich, Germany

GPS Lat: 48.13333 N Lon: 001.58333 E

Grab a stein, step into your *lederhosen* (boys) or *dirndls* (girls), and get ready to drink some of the best brewski in the world at Oktoberfest in Munich. Every fall, huge beer tents are erected in the Theresienwiese meadow for the sixteen days of extreme Bavarian boozing, carousing, and recuperating. Oktoberfest

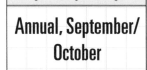

Annual, September/ October

(the two weeks ending on the first Sunday in October)

is the largest annual festival in the world, and over 6 million global visitors have dropped by in recent years.

The large tents can house about 6,000 drinkers at a time and are usually operated by a restaurant or bar owner from town. All the tents serve food and a single brewer's special Oktoberfest beer, and each tent has a slightly different vibe. For example, the Hofbrauhaus Festalle is usually the first stop for tourists, the Hippodrome attracts a more sophisticated crowd, and Festhalle Schottenhamel is where hip, young Germans hang out.

The fun of Oktoberfest begins with a parade featuring the people servicing the tents and brewing the *Wies'n* beer (special Oktoberfest brew). Leading the procession are several teams of huge steeds wearing solid silver, leather, and brass harnesses and pulling colorfully decorated carriages, ornate wagons, waitresses on decorated floats, and various bands. Then the Lord Mayor of Munich, following twelve thundering blasts from the *Wies'n* cannon, taps the first keg of beer, lifts a full stein into the air, and yells, "*Ozapft ist!*" ("It's tapped!"). Waitresses carrying half a dozen or more huge steins with foam sliding down the sides scurry through the masses to quench the thirst of the imbibers.

Aside from the hundreds of tents, each with its own style and decor, there are refreshment stands, exciting and noisy sideshows, fun houses, dancers, rides, shooting galleries, puppet shows, flea cir-

German Information Center

cuses, roller coasters, miniature auto racing tracks, and huge merry-go-rounds.

Beer is served in a huge mug called a *mass*. The revelers suck down over 5 million liters of beer. And they devour hundreds of thousands of grilled chickens and sausages; hundreds of barbecued oxen; tens of thousands of pounds of fish, cheese, smoked tenderloin, ham hocks, spareribs, sauerkraut, and pretzels.

In 1810, Bavarian King Ludwig I married Therese von Sachsen-Hildburghausen. The people of Bavaria celebrated with a sixteen-day party. They had so much fun, they opted to do it again the next year; nearly two hundred years later, they're still at it. Now that's a match made in heaven!

When You Go:

It is impossible to park a car in the vicinity of the Oktoberfest grounds. Public transportation is the best bet, and you don't have to worry about drinking and driving. The U-Bahn (underground), the tram, and taxis are all easy ways to get to the Theresienwiese. Carry only as much cash as you need, as pickpockets have been known to work the tipsy crowd.

> "sixteen days of extreme Bavarian boozing, carousing, and recuperating"

Web Coordinate:

www.whatsgoingon.com/100things/oktoberfest

Anastenaria Firewalking Ceremony

Aghia Eleni, Greece

GPS Lat: 41.08333 N Lon: 023.55000 E

Annual, May 21-23

When you hear the term "Greek firewalking" you may think of a barbaric fraternity hazing rite. But in the small village of Aghia Eleni in the district of Macedonia in northern Greece, firewalking (*pirovassia* in Greek) is something else. It is a serious religious ritual, incorporating a searing dance across hot coals, which attracts incredulous tourists from around the world. Every year from May 21 through 23, the Anastenaria ethnic group holds its annual firewalking celebration.

Firewalking has occurred all over the world for ages, and today it attracts many practitioners and spectators. But Anastenaria Firewalking has a unique twist. Although firewalking may seem paganistic, the Anastenaria people have completely incorporated this bizarre ritual into their Christian religion. This caused the group to be excommunicated from the Greek Orthodox Church for being heathens.

On the evening of May 21, the firewalkers, or Anastenarides, prepare to join God on Earth by meditating, moaning, dancing, and working themselves into a state of spiritual ecstasy. So by the time they begin their barefoot dance into the red-hot embers in a pit in the center of town, the fire is their friend. They emerge on the other side of the coals feet intact, without blisters, burns, or tears.

The dancers hold icons of Saint Constantine and Saint Helen above their heads while crossing the coals. This firewalking ritual began in the year 1250, when some Thracian villagers were said to have rescued icons from a burning church after they heard the icons crying out to be saved. The descendants of these heroic villagers are said to be blessed with the ability to walk on fire. The "proof" is that the firewalkers today purportedly never get burned. To celebrate this amazing feat, a calf is sacrificed after the fire dance.

The Anastenarides hold their festival on May 21, the feast day for Saint Constantine and his mother, Saint Helen. Constantine was a Roman Emperor who "saw the light" and converted to Christianity before his death in A.D. 337. So northern Greek Macedonia is the place to be to see the melding of pagan, Roman, and Christian influences. It's apropos of a region that has been violated throughout history by the Romans, the Byzantines, the Ottoman Turks, and Orthodox Greeks. If you find yourself in Aghia Eleni for the Anastenaria Firewalking Ceremony, don't question the contradictions. Simply work yourself into a state of ecstasy and revel in the unique combination of the pagan and the pious.

Associated Press/California Aggie

When You Go:

When driving northeast from Thessaloniki, stop first in Langadas, 15 miles away; there's a firewalking ceremony there, too. Aghia Eleni is another 30 miles to the northeast, about 9 miles from Serres, the capital of the district of Macedonia. While here, visit the Amphipolis archeological site and the beautiful cave of Alistrati. Cool your feet in therapeutic springs in the nearby villages of Therma and Siderokastro. You may want to travel back to Thessaloniki for comfortable lodging.

"a serious religious ritual incorporating a searing dance across hot coals"

Web Coordinate:

www.whatsgoingon.com/100things/firewalk

Il Palio di Siena (The Palio)

Siena, Tuscany, Italy

GPS Lat: 43.16666 N Lon: 011.31666 E

Dirty fighting. Horses blessed in a church. Rigged betting. Inter-neighborhood fist fights. Amazing food. Hordes of partying tourists. Now *this* is an event!

Annual, July 2 and August 16

The Palio is the roughest and most unruly of horse races. It is held twice each summer and culminates on August 16. The beautiful town of Siena has hosted this bareback romp around the main town square (Il Campo) since 1147. This race is both a spectacle and serious business. It bestows upon one lucky Siena neighborhood, or *contrade*, bragging rights for the whole year.

The Palio is a vestige of ancient Italian rivalries. Siena is carved into seventeen proud contrades. The contrades' competitiveness dates back a millennium, when disputes among them often resulted in battles. Eventually, they put away their swords and settled their differences with horse races around that same battlefield, now one of the most beautiful town squares in the world. But there are still battle-like elements. Jockeys push and shove, bookies try to rig the races, fans sometimes beat up jockeys and taunt horses, and rival spectators come to fisticuffs.

The only rule is that the jockeys cannot grab the reins of other riders. They are allowed to do almost anything else during their three laps around the Campo, and they usually do. It is almost as important for a jockey to keep his contrade's biggest rival from winning as it is to win himself. While jockeys whip rival horses and knock other jockeys down, they must be careful. If a horse finishes first, even without its rider, it wins.

Lot determines which ten of the seventeen contrades will participate in the race each year (those that did not compete last year automatically race). Horses are also chosen by luck of the draw, then are

Italian Government Tourist Board, New York

taken to church to be blessed. The horses often have bowel movements in church, but this is considered to be a good omen.

The Palio is not just wild, it's also a sensual feast involving almost all of Siena's 50,000 citizens in a year-long preparation. All this for a one-and-a-half-minute race! Spectacular Renaissance-style parades start the activities, with the marchers in elaborate costumes and the drums banging. The festivities end with an enormous celebration dinner laid out on a huge table in a Siena street and hosted by the winning contrade. And the people-watching throughout couldn't be better—this is Italy, after all!

When You Go:

Finding a place to watch the Palio isn't easy. You'll have to either stand in a staked-out spot for a whole day before the race begins, or pay a bundle (maybe $100 each) to get a good perch atop the roof of a building on Il Campo. Another option is to head to the street on the southwestern side of Il Campo. From here, you'll be able to shove your way to a spot a couple of hours before the race, along with several thousand other people.

"the roughest and most unruly of horse races"

Web Coordinate:

www.whatsgoingon.com/100things/palio

Venice Biennale

Guardini di Castello, Venice, Italy

GPS Lat: 45.43333 N Lon: 012.33333 E

Take a moment to reflect on the beauty that is Venice. The ancient architecture, the languid canals, the romantic gondolas, and all those pigeons soaring above the Piazza San Marco. How could this masterpiece of a city ever be improved upon? How about by gathering important avant garde art from around the world for a summer-long display? Well, perhaps.

Odd-numbered years, June to October

The Venice Biennale has been a summertime treat nearly every odd-numbered year since its inception in 1893. Despite its long history of good ol' Italian scandal and controversy, the Biennale has endured and remains the best-known and most glamorous forum for contemporary art. Dozens of nations participate by sending their best to be part of the spectacle.

As the debate continues over what is "modern" art, the Biennale has a history of introducing breakthrough schools of thought, from Impressionism and Expressionism at the turn of the century to Pop Art in the 1960s. The Biennale is typically centered around an obtuse theme (the 1997 show's lofty title was "Future, Present, Past"). However, the important feature of the exhibition is that all works are recent and (in most cases) created especially for the Biennale.

While the exhibition is hung in palaces and civic buildings all over Venice, the center of the Biennale is the Guardini di Castello on the eastern tip of the island. Originally laid out by Napoleon, the Guardini is closed to the public except during the Biennale. Over the years, participating nations have built pavilions in the Guardini in which to display their art stars.

Just about every key international artist has made a contribution to the Biennale, from Andy Warhol and Robert Rauschenberg in the 1960s to more recent heavyweights like Jenny Holzer, Mario Merz,

Ann Hamilton, Jeff Coons, and Julian Schnabel.

And what's an art show without awards? A committee of international curators serves up the Biennale's coveted Gold Lion to a living artist, in recognition of his or her contribution to the history of contemporary art.

The Gold Lion awards were disrupted in 1967, when hotheaded artists and students protested the absurdity of giving prizes for art (things were different back then). There were sit-ins in the Guardini, and works in the pavilions were hung upside-down in protest. The awards were quietly reinstated in the 1980s.

Serge Spitzer, Reality Models/Re-cycle 1999

When You Go:

If it takes more than art to satisfy your short attention span, you're in luck. There are also concurrent Biennales for architecture, music, theater, and cinema through the balance of the summer. Plus, there are always dozens of other "Biennale-sponsored" exhibits and art shows scattered about the city. Remember to take along your sensible shoes, and don't show up at the Guardini on Mondays (because the Biennale is closed).

Web Coordinate:

www.whatsgoingon.com/100things/biennale

"the best-known and most glamorous forum for contemporary art"

Venice Carnevale

Venice, Veneto, Italy

GPS Lat: 45.43333 N Lon: 012.33333 E

The Venetian mask is still reminiscent of the Venice Carnevale's traditional fascination with high society, wild decadence, and complete anonymity. Every year, Venetians bring all of these together for the biggest party of the year, just before Lent. Never mind those piddling three-day celebrations—this is a ten-day Italian festival of licentious and raging fun.

Annual, January/February
(the ten days before Ash Wednesday)

Hundreds of thousands of tourists become voyeurs to the self-indulgence that fills the piazzas and alleys of Venice during Carnevale. Acrobats, mimes, street actors, and fire-eaters fill the streets to show off their talents. Costumed revelers use their masked anonymity as an excuse to abandon inhibition, create mischief, and get physical.

All the bawdy behavior pays homage to the even more libertine past of Carnevale. In its famous 1700s decadence, Venetian pre-Lent festivities went on for up to six months. Before the celebration was associated with Lent, Romans celebrated winter with a fertility festival in which masks were worn by princes and slaves alike, abolishing social-class divisions.

Costumes are the essence of Carnevale—and they're extremely expensive and elaborate. Some costumes are fantastic fantasies, but overwhelmingly present are the historic Casanovas, eighteenth-century aristocratic dandies, and medieval figures. Costumes offer the opportunity to immerse yourself in a role. Many locals spend months doing historical research, while the less enthusiastic rent ready-made ensembles and buy masks from local shops.

The clamor of Venice's streets hypnotizes, but take a peek indoors for the full Carnevale experience. Appear in good form at Piazza San Marco's Caffé Florian for late afternoon hot chocolate and you just might get invited to an ultra-exclusive evening ball. The balls not to miss are Ballo Tiepolo, the official eighteenth-century masquerade ball of the festival, and the more sensual Balle del Doge, a forum for the very exhibitionistic. They're expensive at up to $300 a pop, but you can pick from plenty of other affordable, equally frolicsome balls.

Don't miss the cortege on the Grand Canal, featuring a procession of hundreds of decorated boats and gondolas filled with masqueraders (for a price, you can ride along). Make an appearance in Piazza San Marco for the "Flight of the Little Dove," in which a paper dove "flies" on a cable and drops confetti on the crowd below. Young people party in Campo Santa Margherita, and children tear things up at Campo San Polo. It is truly an all-inclusive celebration!

> "a ten-day Italian festival of licentious and raging fun"

When You Go:

Book a room several months in advance—the city fills up fast. When you get there, get a schedule from the tourist office and buy a map, then prepare to be lost. (Learn it now: "*Do've?*" means "Where is?") Don't be dull: rent a costume (or at least buy a mask) from one of the shops around the city. And plan to stop at a bakery and taste *fritola* or *galano*—signature sweets of Carnevale.

Web Coordinate:

www.whatsgoingon.com/100things/carnevale

Italian Government Tourist Board, New York

Cannabis Cup

Amsterdam, Netherlands

GPS Lat: 52.35000 N Lon: 004.9000 E

Annual, November

(Thanksgiving week)

Weed. Grass. Ganja. Herb. Smoke. Pot. Cannabis. Call it what you want, it's just so difficult to make a decision when it comes to marijuana. That's the problem when you sign up to be a judge at the Cannabis Cup, the dopest awards competition around. The Cup is the highest honor that can be given to the little green buds.

For about $200, you get a "judge's laminate," a pass that gets you into the opening and closing ceremonies, coffee-shop tours, concerts, parties, workshops, and "420 Council" meetings and, most importantly, gives you access to lots and lots of weed. No more than 2,000 people can sign up to judge, and they are responsible for voting in categories such as best coffee shop (places that offer cannabis on the menu), best hashish, best hemp product, best hydroponically grown cannabis flower, and best marijuana, which earns the Cannabis Cup.

The criteria for judging the cream of the cannabis crop include appearance, smell, and taste. But the trickiest category to judge is, without a doubt, "effect." Experts say that a well-seasoned judge can handle about five to ten varieties a day.

According to the event's organizer, the venerable *High Times Magazine*, the Cup is "a celebration of the breeders, growers, scholars, and merchants of cannabis." In addition to judging weed, participants can visit the Hemp Expo, hemp fashion shows, concerts, and panels on topics like the uses and controversies surrounding medical marijuana, environmentally correct uses for hemp, and the spiritual uses of marijuana in different cultures.

The spiritual center of the Cup occurs every day at 4:20 P.M., when the 420 Council convenes ("4:20" is the universal stoner catchphrase for "time to smoke pot"). Here, the judges mix with performers, celebrity judges, poets, and speakers in an open forum discussion. All judges are expected to attend the Council, as it is here that any disputes are ironed out, information is dispensed, and the votes are cast.

High Times Archives

The Council begins with a moment of silence and an "Om" prayer, then anyone and everyone is invited to speak his mind.

Also look out for the "Cannabis Hall of Fame Awards," which celebrates people who popularized and humanized cannabis. Inductees are selected by event organizers and have included Bob Marley, Louis Armstrong, Milton Mezzrow, Jack Kerouac, William Burroughs, and Allen Ginsberg.

When You Go:

With all the "judging" required at this event, it is good to know that someone is taking care of the details. Complete tour packages are available that include the coveted judge's laminate, airfare, hotels, admission to all parties and concerts, plus four days of guided coffee-shop tours. While in Amsterdam, don't neglect a trip

> "the dopest awards competition around"

to Sensi's Museum Coffee Shop, home of the Hash, Marijuana, and Hemp Museum.

Web Coordinate:

www.whatsgoingon.com/100things/cannabis

Queen's Day (Koninginnedag)

Amsterdam, Netherlands

GPS Lat: 52.35000 N Lon: 004.9000 E

Can you handle twenty-four hours of nonstop eating, drinking, dancing, and shopping? Every year, Amsterdam's most energetic street party and the world's biggest free market draws the entire local population and thousands of visitors to the streets and canals of this very liberal city. It's all a huge birthday party for the Queen.

Annual, April 30

Amsterdam has the biggest Queen's Day celebration in the Netherlands, but every city or village holds a fair on April 30, called a "free day." All over the country you'll find concerts, formal parties, markets, military parades, children's games, and processions. And everywhere you look, you'll see Dutch flags and orange. People dress in orange, drink "Orange Bitter" liqueur, and yell "Orange Forever!" Sometimes people even paint the national colors on their faces. All this orange obsession does have a reason: The Royal family descends from the house of Orange Nassau.

The party starts on April 29, when up to a million people begin to crowd into Amsterdam. Partiers, live bands, transvestites, and discarded Heineken cups pack the streets. Even on boats in the canals, people drink and sing and make a general ruckus. A big video screen at Centraal Station broadcasts the party and an amazing fireworks show to the crowds.

The next day, Queen's Day, things start buzzing early, as everyone gets busy preparing for the Vrijmarkt (free market), the biggest market in the world. Only on this day, anyone can sell anything on the streets, and street musicians can play without special permission. Thousands of people (including many children) drag out old clothing, books, and records and prepare food to sell to the crowds. In the Vondelpark, one of the main hubs of the celebration, only children are allowed to sell their wares. The market is famous for incredible bargains.

This huge birthday party has been going on every year since 1948, when Queen Juliana succeeded to the Dutch throne as the second Dutch queen. In 1980, Juliana abdicated and was succeeded by her daughter Beatrix, who kept her mother's birthday as a national holiday (hers, on January 31, is too cold). According to tradition, the Queen, her family, and members of the royal house visit two Dutch towns on Queen's Day. The visit is a major occasion, with singing, folk dances, and traditional Dutch games.

> "Amsterdam's most energetic street party and the world's biggest free market"

When You Go:

Amsterdam's semicircular streets can be confusing, so buy a good map. Take a boat tour of the city to get your bearings (it's the best way to see the city). Get to the market early to find the best bargains, and if the crowds get to you, escape to the less crowded outlying neighborhoods. Museums and many stores are closed on Queen's Day, so entertain yourself by renting a bike and riding around the city.

Web Coordinate:

www.whatsgoingon.com/100things/queensday

Netherlands Board of Tourism

Formula One Grand Prix of Monaco

Monte Carlo, Monaco

GPS Lat: 43.73333 N Lon: 007.41666 E

Everyone knows Monaco. Cary Grant and Grace Kelly graced its shores with their charms in Hitchcock's *To Catch a Thief.* And, of course, the beautiful heroine transformed into Princess Grace of Monaco with her storybook wedding to Prince Rainier. Everyone associates Monaco with elegance, nobility, and lots and lots of money.

Annual, May

Once a year the people of Monaco shake things up by staging the most glamorous and challenging auto sports event on the planet. Since 1929, the Formula One Grand Prix of Monaco has offered excitement, sexy cars, and lots of wrecks. The beauty of this Grand Prix event is that it allows viewers to get closer to the action than any other big race in the world. Ferraris and other fine sports cars careen through seventy-eight curvy, death-defying laps around a 3.3-kilometer (2-mile) circuit.

The race occurs right on the streets of the small, usually quiet principality carved into a steep hillside. Of the inaugural race, the magazine *La Vie Automobile* wrote, "It goes without saying that the track is made up entirely of bends, steep uphill climbs and fast downhill runs. Any respectable traffic system would have covered the track with 'Danger' sign posts left, right and centre." Since that first run, the record average speed has jumped from the original record, 80.1 km/hr (about 50 mph), to an amazing 141.7 km/hr (about 88 mph).

A prime spot for you to view the race is right at the start (or *Depart*) of the race. Many of the nastiest accidents occur at the Virage St. Devote, the first bend of the race, where drivers are simultaneously struggling for a position, accelerating, and still adapting to the sharp turns.

The Monaco Government Tourist Board

Otherwise, join the rest of the chic and affluent who idly lounge around on their yachts, in restaurants, and on hotel balconies during the high-strung event. Bask in your bourgeois decadence while you watch the cars zoom around the hairpin turn into the Virage du Portier from a cozy balcony in the Hotel Loews Monte-Carlo, located about halfway through the lap. While you sip your Moët and Chandon, the earnest and brave race drivers hasten around perilous curves below.

You can also watch from the spectator stands, located a bit farther from the action. You won't feel the whoosh as the cars speed past, but you're more likely to avoid being tangled up in the carnage.

When You Go:

If you've got connections and cash, consider watching the action from the most sought-after spot in the principality—the top table at La Racasse restaurant. The Ferraris zip around the scary hairpin bend just inches in front of you. On race day, this table goes for a steep $3,300. If your nerves can't handle the Grand Prix, remember that Monaco also hosts the Annual Mini-Grand Prix for Radio-Controlled Vehicles every October.

> "the most glamorous and challenging auto sports event on the planet "

Web Coordinate:

www.whatsgoingon.com/100things/grandprix

Fatima Pilgrimage

Our Lady of Fatima Basilica, Fatima, Portugal

GPS Lat: 39.61666 N Lon: 008.65000 W

On May 13, 1917, three young peasant shepherds spied a "lady brighter than the sun" sitting in the branches of a tree on the outskirts of Fatima, Portugal. This so-called miracle was the first of six apparitions of the Virgin Mary in the area, which are credited by some as the most famous supernatural occurrence of the twentieth century.

Annual, May 13

Every year on May 13, hundreds of thousands of devout Catholics venture to Fatima by tour bus, donkey cart, and on foot—all to pay homage to Our Lady of Fatima and to perhaps have an apparition of their own. While most Portuguese festivals are full of laughter, singing, and dancing, the Fatima Pilgrimage is an exceedingly austere and massive religious gathering.

The action centers in the giant, central esplanade around the Basilica. In the afternoon, a statue of the Virgin is slowly paraded through the esplanade into the Basilica, and in the evening the faithful hold a candlelight vigil that lasts long into the night. As many people as possible try to cram into the nearby Chapel of the Apparitions, at the location of the alleged appearance. Many of the locals crawl up to the shrine on their knees—quite a poignant and slightly chilling sight.

So what really happened on May 13, 1917? Lucia dos Santos and her cousins, Jacinta and Francisco, were tending sheep when they saw the glowing lady in the tree, who revealed herself as the Virgin Mary. The Virgin told them that she had been sent by God with a message for humanity. To Lucia she revealed the three "Secrets of Fatima." The first was a message of peace and a vision of Hell. The second predicted that Russia would destroy the world, unless the nation was converted to the Catholic faith. The third secret has never been divulged, but Lucia wrote it down on a piece of paper in 1944. The paper is kept in the Vatican, and the third secret is read by each Pope upon his accession. Most believe it foretells of chaos in the Catholic Church beginning in the 1960s.

The Virgin reappeared to the young shepherds on the thirteenth day of each of the next five months, culminating in the so-called "Miracle of the Sun" on October 13. On this day, in 1917, 70,000 people watched the sun dance in the sky above the town of Fatima, then fall to the ground before returning to its normal place in the heavens. This day is celebrated in Fatima with—you guessed it— another pilgrimage.

> "an exceedingly austere and massive religious gathering"

When You Go:

Face it, it's going to be a madhouse in Fatima during the pilgrimage. You are not going to find a place to sleep (much less a place to park or grab something to drink). Consider staying in the beautiful town of Tomar, about 20 miles east of apparition-land. Check out the many kitschy souvenirs at the pilgrimage. A commemorative Our Lady of Fatima ballpoint pen or snow globe might be perfect for your friends back home.

Web Coordinate:

www.whatsgoingon.com/100things/fatima

João Paulo

Hogmanay

Edinburgh, Scotland

GPS Lat: 55.95000 N Lon: 003.21666 W

While it sounds like some kind of porcine rodeo, Hogmanay is actually the boisterous, boozy, soulful, and very Scottish way to ring in the new year. Think of it as a four-day house party, and everyone's invited. Hogmanay literally means "new year"—and remember, these are the folks who gave the world the nearly-impossible-to-remember words and tune of the New Year's theme song, "Auld Lang Syne."

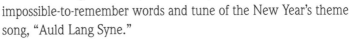

Annual, December 30– January 2

Scotland's capital, Edinburgh, is the center of Hogmanay revelry. However, celebrations take place over just about every square meter of the country. All the activities for Hogmanay in Edinburgh are simply too numerous to mention. Be prepared for concerts, carnivals, balls, fireworks displays, and food festivals. The big highlight on December 30 is a torchlight parade through the city center, culminating with a "fire festival" on Carlton Hill. The fire festival is a pyrotechnist's dream—it combines traditional music, theater, and the torching of huge sets and effigies.

On December 31, the big musical event is the Concert in the Gardens, which features big-name Scottish and international bands. You'll also find hundreds of other musical events around the city, everything from raves to fancy dress balls.

At midnight there are street dances and huge fireworks displays. The church bells ringing until dawn are a constant reminder that the point is to stay up all night.

Another very uniquely Scottish tradition is called "first foot." Scots want the first person who crosses their threshold to bear coal, salt, and whiskey—symbols of warmth, food, and merriment for the upcoming year. Everyone stumbles from house to house, "first footing" and getting progressively more tipsy until dawn.

> "the boisterous, boozy, soulful, and very Scottish way to ring in the new year"

December 31 is the only day of the year in Scotland when pubs are open all night (incidentally, Edinburgh's Rose Street has more pubs per square foot than anywhere else on Earth). More events are planned for January 1, with January 2 being a national holiday specifically for sobering up!

The roots of Hogmanay are obscure and mysterious. Many believe it stems from pagan solstice rituals, and the events involving fire were started as attempts to "bring back the sun," which doesn't make much of an appearance over Scotland in the dead of winter. Interestingly, the first foot ritual—while not familiar to the rest of Europe—is very similar to many Asian new year traditions. Go figure!

When You Go:

It's a good idea to use public transportation during Hogmanay, because Edinburgh will be very congested and most activities are within walking distance. Call the Edinburgh Hogmanay Festival hotline for an up-to-the-minute report on activities (or check out the information boards posted at both ends of Prince Street). And ladies, try to contain yourselves: aside from weddings and funerals, Hogmanay is the only time of the year when most lads don their kilts.

Web Coordinate:

www.whatsgoingon.com/100things/hogmanay

Edinburgh & Lothians Tourist Boards

Up-Helly-Aa

Lerwick, Shetland Islands, Scotland

GPS Lat: 60.15000 N Lon: 001.15000 E

Scotland's remote Shetland Islands play host to a mythic, flaming spectacle like no other on the planet. Didn't you get your invitation? A decision was made years ago to limit visitors so the Shetlanders who run the hotels, restaurants, and shops can attend the festivities. Thus, there is a strict invitation policy to get into most of the dance halls after the notorious procession.

Annual, January 20

The small town of Lerwick burns bright—literally and figuratively—during the notorious Up-Helly-Aa. The fun begins in the early evening of January 20, with a procession down the streets of Lerwick. Nearly one thousand celebrants—some in traditional Viking regalia with winged or horned helmets, shields, and elaborate capes—carry flaming torches down to the appointed burning site. Men in drag, monks in brown habits, cowboys, Indians, hunchbacks, and court jesters abound.

A special group of men, called Guizers, hauls a 30-foot model of a Viking long ship down to the sea front. The longboat is placed on a stand, and the eclectic groups of Nordic revelers solemnly surround the boat. The head honcho, otherwise known as the "Guizer Jarl," gives some Norse signal, a bugle is sounded, and a thousand flaming torches are launched onto the ship.

The ship quickly becomes a blazing inferno, and as if on cue, whiskey bottles are pulled out and toasts are made. Singers burst into a rousing version of "The Norseman's Home," resolutions for the new year are made, and everyone gets nice and wasted. No one is allowed to indulge in any alcoholic intake prior to the burning of the ship for fear that a bunch of inebriated Vikings could set the only town on this Shetland Island ablaze.

After the torching, there are parties at numerous dance halls (a couple of them sell tickets, but most are by invitation), and some of the pubs in Lerwick are open all through the night.

The origin of Up-Helly-Aa is a bit cryptic. Some claim it dates back to a Viking ritual called the New Fire Festival, where the burly invaders attempted to appease the gods by burning things and chanting. Even the root of the name remains somewhat of a mystery. It is clear, though, that this is a New Year's celebration of sorts, with the pyrotechnics meant to help "bring back the sun" and scare away the long winter nights.

> "a mythic, flaming spectacle like no other on the planet"

When You Go:

It's simple! Make some friends in Lerwick, then strongly hint at an invitation for Up-Helly-Aa. Or perhaps the Shetland Island Tourism Office can help you with arrangements and accommodations. If you travel to Lerwick during the summer, the extensive Up-Helly-Aa exhibit at Fort Charlotte (open mid-May through September) may shed some light on the fiery spectacle that is Up-Helly-Aa.

Web Coordinate:

www.whatsgoingon.com/ 100things/uphellyaa

Charles Tait Photographic and Shetland Islands Tourism

Basque Herri Kilorak (Rural Sports)

Bilbao, Spain

GPS Lat: 43.25000 N Lon: 002.93333 W

The Basques say they're the strongest and bravest people in the world. If you visit the Basque Rural Games, you won't even think about arguing! These games, the most brutish and virile of strength contests, are held at the central stadium in Bilbao, Spain, as part of Bilbao's biggest festival, Semana Grande (Big

Annual, August

(during Semana Grande in late August)

Week). The sports, called herri kilorak (or rural sports), stem from agricultural work done in the country since ancient times and are an important tradition in the Basque country. Spend a day with these competitors and you'll find out what testosterone is really all about.

Head straight for the stone-lifting competition. Wearing leather padding, each strongman levers a massive granite and lead stone end-over-end to his chest. Then he boosts it to his shoulder, removes his hands, and whirls around before dropping it onto a cushion. The stone-lifting record is over 325 kilograms (715 pounds)!

Other lifting displays involve speed and are just as fun to watch. In one, the strongman hoists a "measly" 100-kilogram (220-pound) ball to his shoulder and rolls it around his neck using his hands. Whoever maneuvers the stone around his neck the most times in one minute wins. The record is thirty-six times! Another competition measures the number of times a man can hoist a 150-kilogram (330-pound) stone to his shoulder in ten minutes—the record is fifty-two times!

There are also less weighty yet very exciting skill-oriented events. The tug-of-war competition is legendary. A woodcutting competition involves cutting up a row of huge tree trunks as fast as possible. Stone-dragging is done by both oxen and humans, with the objective of covering the longest distance in a set time. In hay-bale throwing, competitors toss hay bales over elevated ropes. In the corn races, each man runs with a 200-pound sack of corn on his shoulder. Then there are contests such as oxcart lifting, grass cutting, milk-can carrying, and ram fights.

> **"the most brutish and virile of strength contests"**

After watching all this, you may not feel very strong and virile. But hey, the Basques have been doing this for centuries. So bury your inferiority complex in the "normal" festivities of Semana Grande, like watching kids walking on stilts and wearing pointed hats, admiring huge papier-maché Don Quixotes, and teasing people in bull suits.

When You Go:

Unless you're seriously muscle-bound, forget about competing. Instead, just enjoy the area, including eating the great food. Local vendors can provide you with greasy cod and a drink called *kaimotxo* (red wine and Coca-Cola). Keep in mind that Basque cuisine is often considered Spain's best. The atmospheric bars in the "Casco Viejo" serve abundant portions of tapas and pintxos. Or you can grab some *manchego* and *salchichon* at the Mercado de la La Ribera, the largest covered market in Europe.

Web Coordinate:

www.whatsgoingon.com/
100things/herri

The Tourist Office of Spain

Las Fallas de Valencia

Valencia, Spain

GPS Lat: 39.48333 N Lon: 000.40000 W

Does the smell of gunpowder excite you? Does the sight of flames make you smile? Well, Las Fallas de Valencia is your kind of event— a smoky, rowdy fiesta where the whole town is set ablaze!

**Annual,
March 15–March 18**

Las Fallas is undoubtedly one of the most unique and crazy festivals in Spain (a country known for unique and crazy festivals). What started as a feast day for St. Joseph, the patron saint of carpenters, has evolved into a five-day, multifaceted celebration of fire. Valencia is usually a quiet city, but the town swells to an estimated 3 million flame-loving revelers during Las Fallas.

Las Fallas literally means "the fires," and the focus of the fiesta is the creation and destruction of *ninots*—huge cardboard, wood, and plaster statues—that are placed at over 350 key intersections and parks around the city on March 15.

The ninots are extremely realistic and usually depict bawdy, satirical scenes and current events (lampooning corrupt politicians and Spanish celebrities is particularly popular). They are crafted by neighborhood organizations and take about six months to construct. Many ninots are several stories tall and need to be moved into position with cranes.

The ninots remain in place until the final evening of the fiesta, when young men with axes chop holes in the statues and stuff them with fireworks. The crowds start to chant, the streetlights are turned off, and all of the ninots are set on fire at exactly the stroke of midnight.

The origin of Las Fallas is a bit murky, but most credit the fires as an evolution of pagan rituals that celebrated the onset of spring and the planting season. In the sixteenth century, Valencia used street-

The Tourist Office of Spain

lights only during the longer nights of winter. The streetlamps were hung on wooden structures, called *parots*, and as the days became longer the unneeded parots were ceremoniously burned on St. Joseph's Day.

Besides the burning of the ninots, there is a myriad of other activities during the fiesta. During the day, you can check out the extensive roster of bullfights, parades, paella contests, and beauty pageants around the city. Spontaneous fireworks displays occur everywhere during the fiesta, but a highlight is the daily *mascleta*, which occurs in the Plaza Ayuntamiento at exactly 2 P.M. When the huge pile of firecrackers is ignited, the ground shakes for the next ten minutes.

When You Go:

Hotel rooms are in short supply during Las Fallas, so plan well in advance. However, great food is plentiful on the streets of Valencia. Older women seem to regard it as their civic duty to fill huge basins with oil and fry up piles of *bunuelos*—absolutely the best donuts on the planet. Another local delicacy, Paella Valenciana, is cooked in huge tins over open fires on street corners.

> "a smoky, rowdy fiesta where the whole town is set ablaze"

Web Coordinate:

www.whatsgoingon.com/100things/lasfallas

La Tomatina

Plaza del Pueblo, Buñol, Spain

GPS Lat: 39.41666 N Lon: 000.78333 W

Annual, August
(final Wednesday)

Splat! Are you prepared to get really messy and slimy? If not, stay away from La Tomatina, a brutal day of sloppy warfare. Twenty thousand warriors crowd into the tiny town of Buñol for the world's biggest food fight. This brief yet king-sized tomato battle is waged in and around Buñol's main square, the Plaza del Pueblo.

La Tomatina began in 1944 as an impromptu small-time tomato fight among amigos and has grown into a huge *guerra* in which the entire town participates. There is no political or religious significance to La Tomatina—it's just good, messy fun. The nearly 90,000 pounds of tomatoes required for the fight aren't even surplus local produce; they're trucked in from Extremadura. (It's a good thing that local goods aren't used—Buñol's chief industry is cement!)

During the morning, shopkeepers keep busy by meticulously covering their storefronts with sheets of plastic. Young Spanish men begin to gather in the square, and rosé wine is passed out to anyone who might want to get liquored up before the hurling commences. Buckets of water are thrown at the crowds as a sort of prologue to the coming mess. The rowdy crowd begins shouting *"tomatos, tomatos, tomatos"* as a series of dump trucks loaded with the ammunition slowly rolls into the square.

What happens next can best be described as a riot of sheer insanity. The people riding in the dump trucks begin pelting the cheering, half-drunken crowd, and then all-out battle ensues. Friends become enemies and strangers become targets as the red bombs are launched through the square. Screams fill the air, and soon the participants resemble extras in a Wes Craven movie. Tomatoes are flying everywhere; no moving object is safe from the barrage. Like a giant Bloody

132

Mary, the streets and gutters are quickly filled with a sleazy, saucy, slippery red ooze.

Like the Geneva Convention, La Tomatina imposes a few rules of engagement. First, you are required to squish tomatoes in your hands prior to throwing them. Throwing bottles or water bombs is prohibited.

In an attempt to bring in more out-of-towners (and, therefore, more targets), the townspeople of Buñol have created a full-blown fiesta around La Tomatina. There are a week's worth of parades, fireworks, and street dances leading up to the big tomato fight. Enjoy!

The Tourist Office of Spain

When You Go:

There are few hotels in Buñol, so plan on staying in Valencia. It's about 30 miles to the west. *Turistas* with cameras or baseball caps are considered prime targets, so dress accordingly. You might even consider taking some science-lab safety glasses to keep tomato shrapnel out of your eyes. The town puts up makeshift public showers down by the river, so you can clean up after the battle.

Web Coordinate:

www.whatsgoingon.com/100things/tomatina

"a brutal day of sloppy warfare"

Running of the Bulls (Los Sanfermines)

Pamplona, Spain

GPS Lat: 49.81666 N Lon: 001.65000 E

Calling all macho, meat-headed, adrenaline-fueled, danger-flirting gringos! Are you interested in staring peril right in its eyes? Do you have something to prove? If so, then come along to every Hemingway-reading frat boy's dream, *Los Sanfermines*, better known as the Running of the Bulls.

**Annual,
July 6–July 14**

Join the thousands of brazen locals and stupid tourists, armed only with rolled-up newspapers, as they frantically scream and run for their lives, only steps in front of the steam rollers with horns. Injuries and death are inevitable, as more than a few runners wind up with horns ripping up their bums, backs, or bellies.

Bull running happens in many other Basque towns, but Pamplona's celebration of survival took a front seat when Ernest Hemingway wrote about it in *The Sun Also Rises*. An estimated 1,000 to 3,000 people run among, around, under, and sometimes on top of the great beasts each day. About three-quarters of the participants are Spaniards, mostly from the Basque region. The serious and most daring are called *aficionados*. You can spot them by their traditional white shirts, white pants, and red scarves tied around their necks and waists. Some loco locals have run the race each year for the past thirty or forty years.

Each morning at 8 A.M., the runners are given the signal and have a thirty-second head start before the bulls are released. Six bulls are let loose each morning. They charge from the corral near the Plaza San Domingo through the streets of the town. Within a few minutes, the bulls reach the end of the course and pour into the bullring, just behind—or in front of—hundreds of runners.

The backdrop for this danger and revelry comes in the form of "sideshows," including a traditional thirteenth-century parade of

134

papier-maché giants and ceremonial presentations of the matadors, culminating with the very best in bullfighting. The Plaza Castillo and the whole town are crammed with partiers and a massive carnival and fair. This celebration is, believe it or not, a family affair. You'll see young people hanging out with their parents and grandparents, all blissfully chain-smoking Ducado cigarettes as one big happy family.

> "every Hemingway-reading frat boy's dream"

Closing ceremonies involve a midnight candlelight procession, giving a sad and solemn conclusion to the mayhem. Papa would be proud.

When You Go:

If you plan on running, it's best to arrive early, about 6 A.M. Experts will advise you to run "with" the bulls, not in front of them. If you fall, don't attempt to get up. Cover your head and wait until the bulls pass. And finally, stay sober. While most people stay up all night drinking before the run, good judgment and alert motor skills could mean the difference between life and death. *¡Buena suerte!*

Web Coordinate:

www.whatsgoingon.com/
100things/bulls

The Tourist Office of Spain

Santa Marta de Ribarteme
"Near Death" Pilgrimage

Las Nieves, Pondreveda, Spain

GPS Lat: 45.25000 N Lon: 008.73333 W

Religious pilgrimages have been a part of Spanish life since the time of the Crusades. But the most morbid and surreal pilgrimage happens in the small Galacian town of Las Nieves. "Near death" and real life merge together here in a **Annual, July 29**

startling stew of Catholicism and paganism in honor of Saint Marta de Ribarteme, the patron of resurrection.

The action that unfolds here can hardly be believed. In short, the pilgrimage is specifically for those who have had a near death experience in the past year. These lucky folk pay their respects to Santa Marta by carrying coffins (or riding in them!) into the church to hear mass.

Thousands of people pour into this tiny town, and by 10 A.M. the streets are clogged with believers and gawkers. The coffins begin to arrive, borne by solemnly dressed relatives carrying their lucky loved ones who have recently escaped death. People without families must carry their own coffins. All proceed toward the small granite church of Santa Marta de Ribarteme. Mass begins around noon and is broadcast outside of the sanctuary so the crowd outside can hear.

When the mass is complete, the church bells ring and a procession of coffins starts up the hill toward the nearby cemetery and then back to circle the church several times. The people begin to chant "Virgin Santa Marta, star of the North, we bring you those who saw death," as a large statue of the saint is removed from the church and carried along with the coffins.

While the sentiment of the pilgrimage is overwhelmingly sober, the scene on July 29 is anything but. There are plenty of Gypsies on hand to entertain, along with brass bands playing enthusiastic *paso dobles* in the town square. And typical of Spanish fiestas, fireworks are ignited everywhere.

Mysterious pagan rites have been part of the culture in Galacia since anyone can remember. Witches, evil spirits, and exorcisms are commonplace here, and it is said that Galacians have always added a bit of "black pepper" to their spiritual beliefs. The Catholic Church has never been able to fully integrate their teachings here, and the spectacle is an attempt to integrate the Church's beliefs with the more "primitive" beliefs of the local inhabitants.

Copyright 1994 Carlos Puga

While you will hopefully never need the services of Santa Marta, it's good to know that the traditions of this pilgrimage are being kept alive. Just in case.

When You Go:

Accommodations are scarce in Las Nieves; consider staying in Vigo. From there, Las Nieves is a two-hour journey by car or bus. Treat this event with respect: While the weather may be very hot, wear something conservative that you wouldn't mind wearing to church. And don't worry about going hungry, because there'll be plenty of street food—the specialty of the day is pungent octopus cooked in copper cauldrons.

> "the most morbid and surreal pilgrimage"

Web Coordinate:

www.whatsgoingon.com/100things/neardeath

Nobel Prize Ceremonies

Stockholm, Sweden and Oslo, Norway

GPS Lat: 59.33333 N Lon: 018.08333 E

Each year on December 10, the most important global gathering of brainiacs and do-gooders convenes to be acknowledged for their achievements to the betterment of mankind. This is the day that the laureates for the Nobel Prizes are recognized in ceremonies at Stockholm's Konserthus and Oslo's Town Hall.

Annual, December 10

Nobel Prizes are awarded in physics, chemistry, physiology or medicine, economic sciences, and literature in Stockholm, while the Nobel Peace Prize is simultaneously awarded in Oslo. The award is anything but paltry—at last count nearly $1,000,000 is split among the recipients of each of the six prizes. Each recipient makes a brief speech to the esteemed audience.

Over the years, the Peace Prize has been awarded to politicians like Teddy Roosevelt, spiritual leaders like the Dalai Lama, organizations like Amnesty International, and regular people. Yes, regular people! In 1997, Jody Williams of Burlington, Vermont, won the prize for her efforts as strategist and spokesperson for the International Campaign to Ban Landmines. She felt a calling and did something about it!

Alfred Nobel, who started the whole thing, was born in Sweden but spent much of his early life in St. Petersburg, Russia. Nobel had a keen interest in chemical engineering and was especially interested in how to harness the explosive power of nitroglycerine; his experiments led to a creation he patented under the name of "dynamite" in 1866.

While extremely talented with explosives, Nobel was also an accomplished poet and writer. He was outspoken on social and peace-related issues and held what were considered radical views in his era. Nobel earmarked $9 million for the fund that annually honors those who have helped the rest of us in some meaningful way.

The festivities in Stockholm beat the ones in Oslo hands down. There is a big parade, followed by a ceremony at Stockholm's Konserthus where His Majesty the King of Sweden hands each laureate a diploma and a medal. It is followed by a luncheon for about 1,300 people at

> "the most important global gathering of brainiacs and do-gooders"

Stockholm's Stadshus, attended by Their Majesties the King and Queen, members of the Royal Family of Sweden, members of the Swedish parliament, and a hand-picked mix of "international guests who represent the sciences and cultural life." The Norwegian ceremony is a much smaller one; only several hundred people attend the luncheon.

When You Go:

Granted, limiting the invitations to "international guests who represent the sciences and cultural life" makes attendance here difficult. However, this invite is also a bit ambiguous. Perhaps you should call your ambassador or make a friend at Cal Tech, which seems to produce many Nobel Prize winners. Or better yet, do something great to better mankind and win your own Nobel Prize. When you accept your medal, remember the proper way to address the King is "His Majesty," and don't attempt to shake his hand unless he extends his first.

Web Coordinate:

www.whatsgoingon.com/100things/nobel

AP/World Wide Photos

139

World Bog Snorkeling Championships

Llanwrtyd Wells, Powys, Wales, U.K.

GPS Lat: 52.11666 N Lon: 003.63333 W

Annual, August
(last Monday,
Bank Holiday Monday)

It takes guts to grab a snorkel and dive into the floating carpet of peat moss, sludge, murk, and slimy whose-a-whats that clog a bog. That's what the World Bog Snorkeling Championships are all about. They happen at the Waen Rhydd Bog in Llanwrtyd Wells, Powys, in Wales, the land of too few vowels. The brave snorkeler who makes the fastest two laps through 60 yards of murky vulgarity wins this event, the yuckiest, muckiest race in the world. If he or she can find the way out, that is.

Coordinators of this charity event cut a channel through the Waen Rhydd peat bog, where audacious competitors get personal with a whole new level of gross. Divers wearing flippers, wetsuits, and snorkels slip down, down, and down into the bog and kick and swim with all the energy they can muster—it takes about two minutes to make it through. The fastest swimmer wins a cash prize and the title of World Champion Bog Snorkeler.

Most bogs look (and sometimes feel) like solid land. Bogs are covered with plants and grasses, but are very water-logged, and when you cut through one, it instantly fills with water. Thus, when the swath is cut through Waen Rhydd, an instant (and filthy) water racing channel is created. What do competitors think of while kicking through the bog? If they're lucky, not of the newts, bugs, and limitless slimy and furry life forms that thrive within.

Hairy creatures aren't all there is to worry about in that black bog. Bogs were once thought of as a place to communicate with gods, goddesses, and dead relatives. As offerings, people tossed in cauldrons, jewelry, and even animal and human sacrifices. It is said that because of the limited amount of oxygen, the bog can preserve bodies sacrificed even 2,000 years ago! The thought of swimming among centuries-old bodies probably makes competitors go faster.

Are you ready to battle the slime, the ooze, the bugs, and the furry-smelly-mossy deposits that are as old as Methuselah? Find out what it takes to be a "bogger" in the small town of Llanwrtyd Wells. If you decide you can't stomach the prospect of lizards in your nose, you can always join the 20-mile Mountain Bike Bog Leaping races happening later in the day.

> "the yuckiest, muckiest race in the world"

When You Go:

Don't forget to pack a snorkel, a towel, and some Q-tips to clear your ears of bog gunk. Llanwrtyd Wells is about 100 miles from London, and if you can pronounce the name, you can ask for directions. When you get there, find Gordon Green, the founder of the event and owner of the Neuadd Arms Hotel. He can give you plenty of bog wisdom and makes a serious breakfast that's included in the price of a room.

Web Coordinate:

www.whatsgoingon.com/100things/bogsnorkeling

Jeff Morgan

The Mid-East and Africa

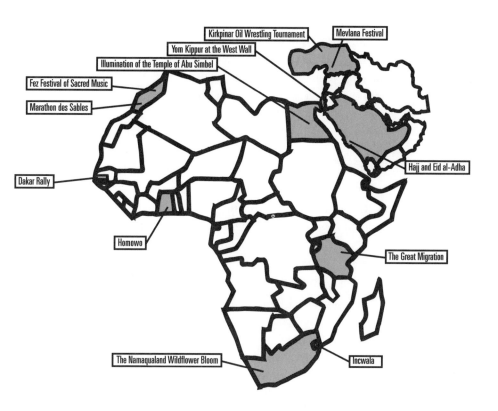

Kirkpinar Oil Wrestling Tournament

Mevlana Festival

Yom Kippur at the West Wall

Illumination of the Temple of Abu Simbel

Fez Festival of Sacred Music

Marathon des Sables

Hajj and Eid al-Adha

Dakar Rally

Homowo

The Great Migration

The Namaqualand Wildflower Bloom

Incwala

Yom Kippur at the Western Wall

Old City, Jerusalem, Israel

GPS Lat: 31.76666 N Lon: 035.23333 E

Yom Kippur is Judaism's most somber and important holiday, taking place on the tenth day of Tishri, the first month of the Jewish lunar calendar. Jews from all over the world go to the Western Wall, also known as *Hakotel* (meaning "The Wall"), on Yom Kippur to atone for their sins of the past year. On this day, God

Annual, September/October

enters the final judgments into his "books." Yom Kippur is the last chance each year for Jews to make their peace with others and then with God.

Hakotel is the last remnant of the Second Temple (destroyed by the Romans in A.D. 70). There is no better place to mark this pious Jewish holiday than at such a holy site. An aura of serenity and peace is maintained even when thousands of holiday worshippers crowd the plaza in front of the Wall, also known as the Wailing Wall.

Repenting begins before sunset the evening before Yom Kippur. After a hearty meal, there is a twenty-six-hour fast that doesn't end until nightfall on Yom Kippur. Washing and bathing are prohibited, as are anointing one's body (no cosmetics or deodorant), engaging in sexual relations, and even wearing leather shoes. Don't be surprised to see the Wall crowded with Orthodox Jews wearing canvas sneakers with their dress clothes.

Jerusalem comes to a standstill on Yom Kippur. No work is done, there are no radio and television broadcasts, and only emergency vehicles are in use. This is the only day on which all Jews (even the most non-religious) truly come together. A hush falls over Jerusalem, and only the echoing of lamentation can be heard.

Most of the day is dedicated to prayer. Different congregations led by their Shaliach Tsibur, or messenger (usually the cantor), take their Torah scrolls to be read at the Wall. A dress code is enforced there;

modest clothing is required, and men and women pray in segregated areas.

After a whole day of prayers, Yom Kippur ends with the *Ne'ilah*, an hour-long prayer that carries a tone of urgency and is sometimes referred to as the closing of the gates—a last chance to get in a good word before the holiday ends. At this final moment God is asked to forgive his people. A very long blast of the *shofar* (a ram's-horn trumpet) signals the end of Yom Kippur and the crowd goes home to a well-deserved dinner.

> "Judaism's most somber and important holiday"

When You Go:

It is customary to wear white on Yom Kippur. Doing so symbolizes purity and the idea that sins shall be made as white as snow. Some people even wear a *kittel,* the white robe in which the dead are buried. Carrying things and writing is not allowed on this day. Therefore, the customary stuffing of cracks in the Wall with paper petitions to God should be saved for another time.

Web Coordinate:

www.whatsgoingon.com/100things/yomkippur

Photo copyright 1999 Israel Ministry of Tourism

145

Hajj and Eid-al-Adha

Ka'ba, Makkah (Mecca), Saudi Arabia

GPS Lat: 21.45000 N Lon: 039.81666 E

Every year, over 2 million people assemble in Makkah for Eid-al-Adha, the festival that marks the end of Hajj, the annual Muslim pilgrimage to Saudi Arabia's Holy City. Muslims make the journey to Makkah (known to westerners as "Mecca") to fulfill the fifth pillar of Islam and to take part in the most significant religious experience of the Muslim world, and therefore of their

Annual, end of March

lives. According to Islamic mandate, Muslims must journey to Makkah at least once if they are physically, mentally, and financially able. With 2 million people packed into such a small place, religious discussion and praise for God intensify the emotional and spiritual experience of pilgrims.

Hajj means "visit to the revered place." Home to the sacred Ka'ba, the shrine Muslims pray toward five times a day, Makkah is so sacred that non-Muslims are not allowed within. Highway signs and armed guards at its borders direct the unfaithful to bypass the city, where even the view is blocked by a wall and by trees against the curious gaze of unwelcome outsiders. Japanese photographer Kazuyoshi Nomachi spent twenty-five years documenting Muslims, and an overwhelming desire to reach the heart of Islam compelled him to convert.

Hajj occurs in the twelfth month of the Muslim lunar calendar, Dhu al-Hijja. It ends with Eid-al-Adha, "The Feast of the Sacrifice." The feast commemorates Abraham's willingness to sacrifice his son Ishmael to Allah, and the mercy God showed them. Worshipers sacrifice an animal in commemoration of the Angel Gabriel's substitution of a lamb for Ishmael. They give one-third of the meat to the poor. The sacrifice reminds Muslims that all humans exist as instruments of Allah. Food, gift-giving to children, and general merrymaking ensue.

Shedding their class-identifying garb, Muslims of all backgrounds dress in seamless white cloth for Hajj to signify their equality in the eyes of Allah. This attitude caused spiritual leader Malcolm X to cast aside his racist views and embrace Islam. Islamic belief states that all religions—Christian, Islam, Jewish—worship the same God.

Hajj pilgrims reenact the last pilgrimage of Muhammad, circling the Ka'ba seven times and traveling seven times between the mountains of Safa and Marwa. Then the pilgrims stand together on the side plane of Arafa and pray for God's forgiveness. The repetitive hike pays homage to Abraham's wife, Hagar, her search for water when left alone by her husband, and the spring that appeared when baby Ishmael kicked the ground in anger. This spring still exists today. It is believed that Allah heals all who drink the water.

> "the most significant religious experience of the Muslim world"

When You Go:

Face it: if you're not Muslim, you're not going. People who make the journey usually plan years in advance. For true believers, religious visas are available at the embassy of Saudi Arabia. Don't take pork, alcohol, explosives, or pornographic materials. If you're a woman, pack some breathable garments for covering yourself from head to toe. Unless you're rich, you'll probably pitch a tent like most other pilgrims. Some travel agencies specialize in arrangements for Hajj.

Web Coordinate:

www.whatsgoingon.com/100things/hajj

Tony Stone Images/Nabeel Turner

Kirkpinar Oil Wrestling Tournament

Edirne, Turkey

GPS Lat: 41.6666 N Lon: 026.56666 E

Every year for more than six centuries, over 1,000 men have gathered in the Kirkpinar Meadow in Edirne, Turkey, to compete in a sweaty, slippery contest of skill, strength, and endurance, the Kirkpinar Oil Wrestling Tournament.

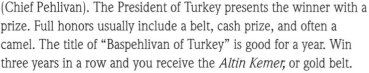

Annual, three days in late June or early July

The goal of the wrestlers, or *pehlivans*, is to become the *Baspehlivan* (Chief Pehlivan). The President of Turkey presents the winner with a prize. Full honors usually include a belt, cash prize, and often a camel. The title of "Baspehlivan of Turkey" is good for a year. Win three years in a row and you receive the *Altin Kemer*, or gold belt.

But it's not easy to get your hands on such prizes. First a pehlivan has to get a grasp on his opponent. Contestants clad only in leather kispet trousers first grease themselves from cauldrons of olive oil and water. Before each match, competitors warm up in front of the referees in a ritual of prayer and chanting, while rubbing their own calves and backs with exaggerated strokes. Finally the contestants shake hands, and the match begins.

Matches are arranged on an elimination basis, and many pairs of wrestlers compete at the same time. There are few rules, but there is a strong code of honor. Wrestlers pride themselves on their gentlemanly conduct. Penalties are given to pehlivans who insult the referee or the spectators with words or gestures, talk or quarrel with their opponents during the contest, don't behave seriously, or try to fix the tournament.

How did such an unusual tournament begin? Legend has it that forty soldiers who had just captured some towns decided to make camp. But they were too pumped from their conquests to relax, so they decided to wrestle. Two of them wrestled for a very long time, but neither could win. Rather than calling it a draw, they kept

Turkey Ministry of Tourism

wrestling and wrestling. Finally, at midnight, the two tough souls ran out of breath and died. Their bereaved friends buried them under a fig tree. Visitors to their graves discovered a spring of water coming from between the two tombstones and called it *Kurklar Pinari*, meaning "The Spring of the Forty." Over time the name changed to "Kirk Pinar," but the wrestling tradition was maintained. Oil is used now because it is believed that it levels the playing field and causes each pair to wrestle longer, in the spirit of the original match.

When You Go:

Get ready for a journey. From Istanbul, head 235 kilometers (146 miles) across highway E5 through the Balkans to Edirne. This costs a mere $3.50 by bus. On the outskirts of Edirne, transfer to a city bus for the final leg. After finding a place to stay, get in the local spirit by chowing down on a local staple, *koc yumurtasi* (ram testicles). Tell them to hold the *zeytinyagi* (olive oil)—there'll be plenty of that later on! While in Edirne, visit the fabulous Mosque of Selimiye.

Web Coordinate:

www.whatsgoingon.com/100things/oilwrestling

"a sweaty, slippery contest of skill, strength, and endurance"

Mevlana Festival (Whirling Dervishes)

Konya, Turkey

GPS Lat: 37.85000 N Lon: 032.50000 E

Annual, mid-December

What exactly is a whirling dervish? The term is tossed around all the time. If you drop by southern Turkey in December, you can find out by catching a glimpse of the real thing.

Each year, there is a week-long celebration in Konya in which members of the mystical Sufi Dervish Order gather in a beautiful, dizzying religious rite to spin their way toward a closer union with God. The Dervishes whirl only once a year (yes, they do have day jobs), so timing is critical if you want to do some whirling observing.

The Dervishes consider their whirling a way to pull cosmic energy to Earth. And who couldn't use a little extra cosmic energy? The ceremony is pretty simple—men of the Order don long white robes with full skirts, black cloaks, and tall conical red hats (which, incidentally, are meant to represent their tombstones). The ritual begins as the Dervishes pass by a religious mystic called a *seyh*, who whispers secret orders.

Then the dervishes start twirling in unison, to the accompaniment of drums and reed flutes, called *ney*. As they spin faster, they raise their right hands up to receive the blessings of heaven and put their left hands down to give the blessings to the earth. In Turkish, this is known as the *sema*. The goal of the dancers is to achieve a state of ecstasy and to relinquish their ties to the physical world. When the music suddenly stops, the Dervishes kneel down. The dance is then repeated two more times. Then the *hafiz* (a man who has memorized the entire Koran) closes the ceremony by reciting passages from the holy book.

Beginning as a religious order in the thirteenth century, the Dervishes survive today as a cultural brotherhood. The Order was founded by Mevlana Jalaluddin Rumi, an Islamic poet who wrote of tolerance, forgiveness, and enlightenment. The whirling ceremony is held on the anniversary of Mevlana's "wedding night" with God. Today, the green-tiled mausoleum of Mevlana is still Konya's most prominent building.

Turkey Ministry of Tourism

Attached to the mausoleum, the former Dervish seminary now serves as a museum housing manuscripts of Mevlana's works and artifacts related to the mysticism of the Order. Although the Dervish mannequins in the museum don't whirl at the touch of a button, they help you feel the awe and spirituality of the Order.

When You Go:

Konya is more than a 650-kilometer (400-mile) drive from Turkey's biggest city, Istanbul. An important pilgrimage center for Turks, Konya usually is very crowded (over one million people visit each year). The good news is there are plenty of lodging options to accommodate any budget. It's also a very conservative town, so men should refrain from wearing short pants, and women should take a long-sleeved blouse and a skirt long enough to cover their ankles.

Web Coordinate:

www.whatsgoingon.com/100things/dervish

"a beautiful, dizzying religious rite"

Illumination of the Temple of Abu Simbel

Abu Simbel, Nubia, Egypt

GPS Lat: 22.36666 N Lon: 031.63333 E

Annual, February 22 and October 22

Pharaoh Ramses II was a prolific builder. His biggest accomplishment was a massive temple carved into a mountain on the Nile River, in Abu Simbel. It's home to an amazing biannual occurrence that reveals an astounding scientific achievement, demonstrating how advanced ancient Egyptians really were. The temple faces east at such a precise angle that, twice a year in the early morning, the sun slowly creeps into the cavernous temple through its large chambers and narrow halls, illuminating the inner sanctum.

The illumination occurs on February 22 and October 22, celebrating Ramses' birthday and coronation, respectively. For only a few hours, the back wall of the innermost shrine is illuminated, mystically lighting up three statues that remain in darkness for the rest of the year. The three statues—Ramses and the sun gods Re-Horakhte and Amon-Re—are in the company of the Theban god of darkness, Ptah (appropriately, he remains in the shadows all year).

At sunrise on the days of the illumination, hordes of people gather at the Temple to watch the sun creep in. Outside, a special fair and folk dancing entertain everyone when the sun's rays are out of range of the inner chamber.

The facade of the Temple is carved with four giant statues of Ramses and mini-statues of members of his family—his mother, son, and favorite wife Nefertari. Inside, the floor gradually rises and the roof lowers as you travel chamber by chamber into the depths of the temple toward the sanctuary. Wall carvings depict Ramses and Nefertari. Even though Ramses was a ladies' man with several wives and over one hundred children, Nefertari was his favorite woman. She

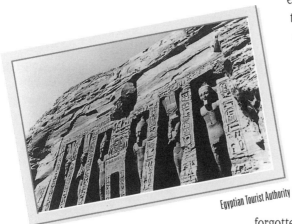

Egyptian Tourist Authority

even gets her own temple, located around the corner from Ramses' pad. Besides the nifty illumination, the coolest thing about the Temple of Abu Simbel is its dramatic history. The temple was forgotten when Christianity was adopted in Egypt and wasn't rediscovered until 1813. In the 1960s, when the Nile was dammed and Lake Nasser almost submersed the Temple, UNESCO pioneered a rescue. They broke it into pieces, removed the chambers imbedded in the mountain, and moved the entire temple (with pieces weighing up to 30 tons) up and back.

The only by-product of the move is that the days of illumination have shifted by one day (February 21 and October 21 are the real days of his birth and coronation). Not bad!

When You Go:

Abu Simbel used to be an easy day trip from Aswan, but nowadays the road is sometimes closed off due to threats of terrorism (and, some say, as a way to generate more money). Now you must fly from Aswan to Abu Simbel. Or you can take the river less traveled and do the less touristy three-day trip by boat down the Nile to Lake Nasser. Take the appropriate precautions for malaria, yellow fever, and hepatitis before you go.

> "an amazing biannual occurrence that reveals an astounding scientific achievement"

Web Coordinate:

www.whatsgoingon.com/100things/abusimbel

Homowo (Hunger Hooting)

Accra, Ghana

GPS Lat: 05.55000 N Lon: 000.25000 W

Forget about simply singing for your supper; head for Accra, Ghana, to join thousands of people in "hooting at hunger." All of the whoopin' and a-howlin' is part of the Ga tribe's Homowo, a summer festival celebrating the harvest season and one of the most joyful festivals in Africa. Visitors are especially honored,

Annual, August/September

so before you know it, you'll be communing with spirits and dancing with the Thursday people.

Homowo, which means "hooting (or jeering) at hunger," is the most important Ga festival, marking the Ga new year. The festival began hundreds of years ago during a famine, which the gods ended in answer to a lot of hooting. Each year, the Ga hoot to ask the gods to continue to sustain them. The two months of celebration include special dances, singing, ancestor worship, and bull slaughters to offer thanksgiving to the area's ninety-nine dieties. The festivities culminate on a Saturday chosen as "Homowo Day," the most sprited day of Homowo.

Throughout Homowo, traditional priests perform "yam festivals," going into wild trances to channel *dzeman wojin*, or supernatural beings. Also, Ga people believe the human spirit exists long after death. At cemeteries, priests sprinkle food and alcoholic beverages in tribute to ancestors. During Homowo, misunderstandings and feuds among families and friends are settled. In preparation for *sisai adjoo* (a "ghost dance" with ancestors), all drumming is banned, in order to usher in the spirits.

Each year on the Thursday before Homowo Day, every Ga journeys back to Accra, the Ga ancestral home. Thousands of pilgrims arrive, carrying baskets of newly harvested vegetables on their heads. Everyone in Accra gathers for their arrival, yelling, "*Soobii*!" ("Thurs-

Obo Addy, Homowo African Arts and Cultures

day people!"). On Friday, a priest honors twins (and other multiple births). Multiple births are considered to be special creations of God. Mothers smear whitish clay on the bodies of their twins, preparing them for a special meal of yam with eggs and asking the gods to bless the souls of their young children.

On Homowo Day, Ga women prepare a special Homowo dish for visitors who stop by. At noon, the paramount ruler of the Ga, Ga Mantse, walks through the town tossing *kpokpoi* (a gloppy mixture of okra and corn) into the air, offering it to the gods, while celebrants throng around him, hooting energetically.

You keep saying that it's time you gave a hoot about something. So this summer head for Ghana, where hooting is a way of life, tossing food is acceptable, and you can dance like the wind with your great-great-great-grandpappy.

> "a summer festival celebrating the harvest season and one of the most joyful festivals in Africa"

When You Go:

You know the drill: tetanus, hepatitis A, and typhoid vaccinations and malaria precautions. Sunblock is expensive in Ghana, so take some along—it's very sunny and hot. For authentic Ga food, take a walk to the Makola Market, a huge West African bazaar in Accra. Take your own bowl, knife, and fork (to be sure you're eating with clean utensils). When you're not hooting, head to the beach nearby to cool off and rest your lungs.

Web Coordinate:

www.whatsgoingon.com/100things/homowo

Fez Festival of World Sacred Music

Fez, Morocco

GPS Lat: 34.08333 N Lon: 005.00000 W

The city of Fez, Morocco, is the perfect place for the Festival of World Sacred Music. The walled city takes pride in its artistic and intellectual heritage, and especially the centuries of peaceful coexistence of its communities of Christians, Jews, and Muslims. That's why it's the home to the most diverse and enlight-

Annual, end of May

ened musical gathering in the world, bringing together the spiritual music of religions worldwide.

The top sacred music artists from eastern, mid-eastern, and western religious communities gather in Fez for a week of concerts, lectures, exhibitions, and intellectual and artistic exchanges. Performances are very diverse and have included the Sufi Whirling Dervishes of Turkey, Berber trance music, Arab-Andalusian music, Javanese Gamelan, Hindustani chants, Celtic sacred music, Christian Gospel, flamenco, and the Philharmonic Orchestra of Morocco. The musicians, young and old, are a part of a groundbreaking effort to bridge cultural differences through musical expression.

Styles of spiritual music at the Fez Festival vary from transcendent to trance inducing. Music can claim to hold curative properties, convey religious teachings, praise God, or channel the spirit of the deities. Some music traditions are centuries old, while others are relatively new; some are serious, and others joyful. But despite the vast differences between the cultures, all at the Fez Festival of World Sacred Music have come for one reason: to share the way in which music allows them to commune with their higher power.

Most of the people who attend the festival concerts are wealthy Moroccans, although a handful of western tourists enroll in planned tours or just show up and dish out roughly $300 for tickets to festival performances. The Crown Prince of Morocco has been known to attend the performances, which have been staged in the King's palace reception court, the Moorish Palace, the Batha Museum, and even the nearby Roman ruins of Volubilis. The Opening and Closing Ceremonies are a little more expensive, but they're usually the most spectacular and are well worth it.

When the concrete starts closing in and the pollution begins to choke, a little jaunt to the Festival of World Sacred Music might be just what the doctor ordered. Take a break from the "civilized world" of technology and industry and head for Fez. We can all use a little more spirituality.

When You Go:

It's hard to navigate the labyrinthine streets of Fez and to deal with all the people hassling you to buy carpets and souvenirs. Enlist the help of a guide. There are two kinds: aging *djellaba*-clad "official" guides who are boring, and illegal Ray-Ban-clad "student" guides who are often very entertaining. We know you'll make the right choice. Watch out, though. Everybody wants to take you to their cousins' carpet stores. You can plan a trip yourself that is much cheaper than taking a tour, but if you like the security, a few tour groups organize trips to the Fez Festival of World Sacred Music.

Web Coordinate:

www.whatsgoingon.com/100things/sacredmusic

Sarah Tours, Inc.

Marathon des Sables (Marathon of the Sands)

Near Ouarzazate, Morocco

GPS Lat: 30.95000 N Lon: 006.83333 W

Annual, April

It could be your ultimate test of endurance or your worst nightmare. The Marathon des Sables is one of the world's most brutal foot races—a six-day, 250-kilometer (150-mile) run through the Sahara Desert in southern Morocco.

Who would be crazy enough to sign up for this torture test? Evidently, lots of people. Nearly 500 brave men and women from twenty-six countries usually step up to the challenge (and most of them actually finish). The competitors range in age from sixteen to seventy-four years old and have included former gold medal Olympians, polar explorers, executives, scientists, homemakers, and a yogi.

Participants are required to be totally self-sufficient during the marathon. They must carry lightweight backpacks with all the clothing, food, and supplies they will need for the week. Marathon organizers supply the runners with a measly 9-liter ration of water for each day. At night, participants sleep on the ground in communal Berber tents.

The actual course and location of the race remain a secret until the day before the marathon begins. Typically, it takes place in the stunningly beautiful desert to the east or south of the town of Ouarzazate. This arid terrain offers an ankle-wrenching variety of landscapes, including rocky hills, palm groves, dried mud flats, and sand dunes. Daytime temperatures have been known to climb to a scorching 125 degrees, and sandstorms are not uncommon.

Each day of the marathon is an adventure unto itself, as each of the six "stages" ranges from 20 to 60 kilometers (12 to 38 miles) in length. An extensive road book is given to the competitors before the race begins. Stage Four is considered the most grueling, a double

158

Jennifer Murray

marathon segment that begins long before sunrise. The racing is tightly monitored, with all participants required to check off at numerous "control points" along the way.

The marathon is littered with stories of survival. Take Mauro Prosperi, a police officer from Rome who got lost in a sandstorm during the 1994 race. He wandered several hundred kilometers off course and survived for the next nine days on boiled urine and dead bats. Mauro lost over thirty pounds during his ordeal but has returned to Morocco to race two more times. Surprisingly, only one person has died while participating in the Marathon des Sables.

When You Go:

It costs about $2,500 to participate in the Marathon des Sables (the winner receives about $4,500 and a coin-sized medal). You'll also need a medical certificate from your physician and results from an EKG test. When you fill out the entry form, pay special attention to the section concerning the "corpse repatriation fee." During the race, if you become severely dehydrated and require an IV more than once, you'll be disqualified.

"one of the world's most brutal foot races"

Web Coordinate:

www.whatsgoingon.com/100things/marathon

Dakar Rally

Europe to Dakar, Senegal

GPS Lat: 14.63333 N Lon: 017.45000 W

Since 1979, the world's most hardened racers have been getting their thrills at the grande dame of all off-road racing events, the Dakar Rally. Three hundred or so car, truck, and motorcycle diehards race in different classes in this eighteen-day test of endurance. The trek usually starts in well-paved Paris, heads south

Annual, December 31 to mid-January

into Northern Africa, and winds up on the dirt roads of Dakar, on the coast of Senegal—at least for those lucky enough to live through the race and not break down. Only about one-third of the racers finish.

The rally route changes each year but always ends up ripping through Africa. Countries along the route have included Algeria, Niger, Mali, Senegal, Upper Volta, Cote d'Ivoire, Mauritania, Morocco, Sierra Leone, and Libya. Racers have to traverse blistering desert, enormous sand dunes, rock outcroppings, and hidden mountain passes.

Each daily stage of the Dakar Rally covers a different route. Stages are around 350 miles, but length depends on the terrain. A route book is provided to competitors the day before each stage, illustrating especially tricky areas, but reconnaissance or test sessions are forbidden. The racer with the lowest accumulated stage times wins.

Often, service access to the drivers during the most difficult stages is forbidden, to even the chances for corporate and individual teams. Emanuelle Surun, one of the coordinators, says that "This makes it a little more even and gets the race back to basics—make it through the desert alive and finish."

One thing the organizers cannot regulate is whether the racers get shot at by desert desperados or unfriendly armies, as has happened in the past. As Surun makes clear, "The drivers know what they are signing up for. They know they could get lost, their car could blow up from heat, whatever." But they keep returning, partly for the thrill of the race, and partly for the camaraderie at the campsite each night, where competitors, mechanics, the press, and the locals all mingle.

The Dakar Rally was the dream of Frenchman Thierry Sabine. His creation was an instant hit. But during the first Rally, a driver fractured his skull and died. Since then, accidents have been part of the Dakar Rally, and approximately three dozen people have died. Sadly, during the Rally of 1986, Thierry died in a helicopter crash while rushing to an accident scene. His death was a shock but, as Thierry would have wanted, the race went on.

> "the grande dame of all off-road racing events"

When You Go:

Over much of the route, unless you're a local, you're not going to be welcomed with open arms. You've also got to watch out for land mines, border conflicts, and other minor impediments. However, if you dare to scoff at all this and have a death wish, a vehicle to spare, the entry fee (of about $10,000), and some good friends to help you, then you, too, can probably race in the Dakar Rally. Just apply, pay up, and hope you get accepted. You may be rejected at the discretion of the organizing body or if there are too many entries. And you must race for the thrill of competing, not for the money, as the prize is less than the entry fee!

Web Coordinate:

www.whatsgoingon.com/100things/dakar

Photo courtesy Thierry Sabine Organization

Namaqualand Wildflower Bloom

Namaqualand, South Africa

GPS Lat: 29.50000 S Lon: 022.0000 E

For eleven months out of the year there isn't much of a reason to visit South Africa's Namaqualand region. This arid, desolate, and sparsely populated area 200 miles north of Cape Town is home to nomadic Afrikaner sheep herders. Europeans didn't settle into the area until around 1850.

Annual, mid-August to mid-September

However, for a few weeks each springtime, Namaqualand's expansive mountain deserts host one of nature's most shockingly brilliant floral displays. The usually barren landscape becomes covered with a carpet of multihued wildflowers. Over 4,000 varieties of flowering plants participate in this visual explosion of color, including Namaqualand Daisies (*Dimorphotheca sinuata*), aloes, lilies, mesembryanthemums, vygies, and perennial herbs. All the flowers create a vibrant patchwork of purple, yellow, orange, and white.

This colorful display is a notoriously fickle one. It is impossible to tell when and where the bloom will begin, as the show is dependent on rainfall, wind, sun, and temperature. Some years are better for viewing than others, and the best viewing spots vary from day to day. Due to the region's vastness, the prime viewing areas can be miles apart.

There are a few things you can count on when visiting the bloom, though. Most of the flowers are light sensitive, so they open up around 10 A.M. and close around 4 P.M. Rainy, windy, or cloudy weather inhibits the show. Since the flowers always face the sun, it is best to view them from the east in the morning and from the west in the afternoon.

A car is essential when visiting the Namaqualand bloom because the distances between the fields are often great and the wildflowers are so unpredictable. Plan on spending a lot of time behind the wheel while you stalk down the best sites. Be flexible, carry a detailed map, and think of the experience as a wildflower safari—sometimes you will find your prey and sometimes you won't. When you do find that amazing patch of wildflower Nirvana, by all means get out of the car and take a hike through nature's temporary tapestry.

> "one of nature's most shockingly brilliant floral displays"

Although viewing the flowers of Namaqualand may sometimes prove to be an elusive experience, the reward is well worth the hassle. Just remember this famous local line: "In Namaqualand you weep twice—once when you first arrive and once when you leave." Happy hunting!

When You Go:

Check with local tourist offices a few days before your flower trek to confirm the optimal locations to see the bloom. Carry extra drinking water and fill up your gas tank before you go. Pack a picnic, as there will be nowhere to dine. If the weather isn't great when you get there, take a drive down to the coast or learn about the local history at the museums in nearby Vanrhynsdorp or Springbok.

Web Coordinate:

www.whatsgoingon.com/100things/namaqualand

South African Tourism

Incwala (Festival of the First Fruits)

Mbabane, Swaziland

GPS Lat: 26.33333 S Lon: 031.13333 E

The new year comes a little early in Swaziland, and it is celebrated with one of the biggest and most intricate African festivals. Incwala, or "Festival of the First Fruits," brings the country together to gain the blessing of ancestors, sanctify the kingship, and kick off the harvest season with a rockin' party. The two

Annual, December

main celebrations are Little Incwala and Big Incwala. Dates are firmed up by tribal astronomers just weeks before.

The festival begins at "no moon," when people of the Bimanti clan (water people) trek to the Indian Ocean off Mozambique to collect the foam of the waves, which is believed to have mystical powers. They return to the king's royal cattle *kraal* (palace), and at dawn of the new moon, the king chews sacred foods (prepared with the foam) and spits them to the east and west. Then Little Incwala begins. For two days, the people wear traditional outfits and chant sacred songs while the king remains in his kraal.

Big Incwala begins at the full moon. It reflects the maturity of the king—the more mature he gets, the wilder the party. The first day, young men walk over 25 miles to gather branches of the sacred Lusekwane bush by the light of the full moon. If any of the men ever made love to a married woman or made a young maiden pregnant, the branches will tell all. It is believed that leaves that touch his unpure hands will wither, and the "pure" people will beat him. Back at the king's kraal, locals sing and drink traditional beer.

On the third day of Big Incwala, young men slaughter an ox and warriors perform the *inczuala* dance around the enclosure where the king hides, begging him to emerge. Eventually the king returns to his people in full Incwala dress. He performs a sacred dance, then eats the first pumpkin of the harvest. When he tosses the rind, the crowd performs a sacred song and dance, and then it's okay to eat the first fruits with the blessings of Swazi ancestors.

After a day of rest and meditation, the celebrants build a huge bonfire to burn articles representing the past year, including the king's bedding and other household items. The Swazi people pray to their ancestors to bring rain to put out the fire, and then the big celebration of the new year starts, with feasts, singing, and dancing. Let the party begin!

> "one of the biggest and most intricate African festivals"

When You Go:

Swaziland is located in a little pocket east of South Africa—the king's cattle kraal is in the vicinity of the cities Mbabane and Lobamba. Keep in mind: getting around isn't easy. Also, food and waterborne diseases cause lots of illnesses in travelers in southern Africa, so be extra careful (iodine tablets purify water). Take lots of insect repellent and a long-sleeved shirt and pants to wear between dusk and dawn, to ward off malaria-carrying mosquitoes.

Web Coordinate:

www.whatsgoingon.com/100things/incwala

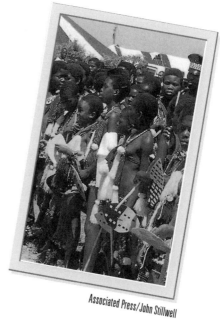

Associated Press/John Stillwell

Great Migration

Serengeti National Park, Tanzania

GPS Lat: 02.33333 S Lon: 034.83333 E

When it comes to wildlife, the Serengeti National Park in Tanzania is the place to be. The 5,700 square miles provide a habitat for over 3 million animals and are home to the most amazing wildlife migration in the world. Every year when the Serengeti's rainy season ends, over a million wildebeest begin an annual pil-

Annual, May through September

grimage in search of food. They are joined by hundreds of thousands of zebras, antelopes, and gazelles and hundreds of hungry lions.

Humans travel by safari to the Serengeti to watch the amazing natural event. (Some even watch from above, in a hot air balloon!) You can observe the wildebeest milling around before their journey begins or as they travel across the plains, flanked by hunting lions. As the hundreds of columns of wildebeest advance, lined up nose to tail, they stretch as far as the eye can see—a breathtaking sight!

Wildebeest are always on the move: In their annual circular jour-ney they cover over 1,500 miles looking for food and water. The ani-mals follow migration routes defined by ages of collective experience. They live fifteen years or more, constantly teaching the route to the young. When the rainy season ends in May, the million beasts gather and prepare to travel west then north to find grazing land. By August, they are out of the Serengeti and in Kenya's Masai Mara Park, whose pastures offer vital sustenance.

When the wildebeest exhaust the resources of the Masai Mara and the Lamai Wedge in the north, they travel south, back to the Serengeti. Chance determines whether their crossing of the wide Mara River is safe, at a shallow point, or whether it's impeded by a high river or steep banks. If they are unlucky, hundreds of wildebeest drown in the river, becoming food for the circling vultures above, or are grabbed and eaten by excited crocodiles. The wildebeest remain in the Serengeti National Park until May, when they begin their journey north again.

The name Serengeti comes from the Masai word for "endless plains," a truly fitting description. Over thirty-five species of plains mammals live in the park, from warthogs to baboons to elephants to cheetahs. Many are unique to the Serengeti. The migration of the wildebeest is one of the world's rare undisturbed migrations, literally defining the ecosystem of the park and surrounding areas. It preserves the delicate balance of the food chain essential to the ecosystem.

> "the most amazing wildlife migration in the world"

When You Go:

Nature lodges and safaris set up specifically for the migration can be expensive, but the experience of guides is invaluable. A few campgrounds offer a place to pitch a tent, but it's very dangerous for inexperienced travelers to go alone. Take light clothing for hot days and a light jacket for nights, good shoes, sunscreen, and insect repellent (malaria exists here). Don't forget to pack lots of film, which is very expensive in Tanzania.

Web Coordinate:

www.whatsgoingon.com/100things/migration

George McBean

India and Asia

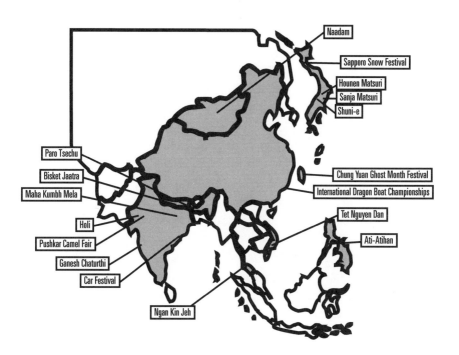

Naadam

Sapporo Snow Festival

Hounen Matsuri

Sanja Matsuri

Shuni-e

Paro Tsechu

Bisket Jaatra

Maha Kumbh Mela

Chung Yuan Ghost Month Festival

International Dragon Boat Championships

Holi

Tet Nguyen Dan

Pushkar Camel Fair

Ati-Atihan

Ganesh Chaturthi

Car Festival

Ngan Kin Jeh

Ganesh Chaturthi

Chowpatty Beach, Mumbai (Bombay), Maharastra, India

GPS Lat: 18.93333 N Lon: 072.85000 E

Come celebrate the birthday of Lord Ganesh. He's the roly-poly, elephant-boy superhero who rides around on a mouse. He's also the ruler of all things auspicious and successful, so it pays to treat him well!

Annual, August/September

For the several months prior to Ganesh Chaturthi, sculptors in the nearby villages of Pune and Pen work overtime to create hundreds of thousands of clay idols of Ganesh. Truckloads of idols in every size, pose, and color are taken into Mumbai to be worshipped in homes, stores, and businesses. The idols are painted and dressed with delicate clothes and jewelry by Ganesh's devotees.

The biggest public culmination of Ganesh Chaturthi happens on Chowpatty Beach in a large-scale immersion. The city comes to a standstill as hundreds of thousands of worshipers crowd the beach and gawk at huge figures of Ganesh. As these king-sized idols are dragged into the sea, the crowd goes wild and shouts the chant "Ganapati Bappa Morya." The scene is a show of religious fervor at its highest intensity, and along with the big immersion ceremony, there are processions, music performances on beautifully decorated stages (called *pandaals*), cart races, and wrestling matches.

The Chowpatty gathering was first organized in 1892 by freedom fighter Lokmayna Tilak. His intent was to use the holiday's appeal as a way to propagate the struggle for independence and to circumvent British anti-assembly legislation.

According to Hindu mythology, Lord Ganesh was immaculately "created" with bath oils by the goddess Parvati, who then sent him outside to guard the house while she was bathing. When his "father" Lord Shiva came home, Ganesh would not let him into the house, so Shiva got angry and cut off his head. As you can imagine, Parvati was furious with her husband and told him to take the head of the first sleeping animal he saw to put on the body of his son. He came back with the head of a baby elephant.

Good thing he chose an elephant: Ganesh's big elephant head symbolizes lots of knowledge. His big ears symbolize the ability to listen. His trunk shows his gift for smelling the good and bad in people. Finally, his small beady eyes symbolize the ability to see the future and what is real in life.

When You Go:

Get over any fear of crowds you may have—during Ganesh Chaturthi, you will be awash in humanity. Wear comfortable clothing, and don't take along anything you would mind losing. The area around Chowpatty Beach will be utterly gridlocked, so be prepared to walk a mile or two in order to get there. And remember, there's still a bit of politics involved—Hindu extremists have caused some trouble here in recent years, so be on your guard.

Web Coordinate:

www.whatsgoingon.com/100things/ganesh

India Tourist Office, New York

Rath Yatra (Car Festival)

Jagannath Temple, Puri, Orissa, India

GPS Lat: 19.81666 N Lon: 085.90000 E

In an English dictionary, the word "juggernaut" is defined as an "irresistible destructive force." This term was coined by British settlers in India when they witnessed the annual spectacle at the mighty Jagannath Temple.

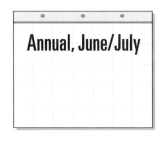

Annual, June/July

Rath Yatra, or the Car Festival, is recognized as one of the most stupendous and fanatical processions anywhere on the globe. The starting point is the twelfth-century Jagannath Temple, which looks something like an antique rocket ship and towers to a height nearly 200 feet above the town. For Hindus, the temple is one of the four holy *Dhams*, or "abodes of the Divine," and millions of pilgrims come each year to pay homage to the deity Lord Jagannath, Lord of the Universe.

The temple houses wooden effigies of Jagannath, his brother Balabhadra, and his sister Subhadra. During the Car Festival, each of the effigies is put in its own giant chariot, or *rath*, and pulled through the center of town on Grand Road to their summer residence, the *Gundicha Ghar*, about a mile away. After the nine-day holiday, the procession is reversed and the gods are returned to their primary residence.

The chariots are huge wooden structures that are built each year to exacting specifications (after the festival, the chariots are dismantled and the wood is used in the temple's communal kitchens and to fuel funeral pyres). These raths are over 40 feet high, and their sets of sixteen carved wheels are nearly 8 feet in diameter. Each of the chariots is preceded by four intricately carved wooden horses.

Lord Jagannath has the tallest chariot, which is covered with red and yellow bunting. Balabhadra's rath is the one with the green bunting, and Subhadra's is covered in black.

The chariots are pulled with thick ropes by 4,200 workers from the temple (which employs 20,000 people). The devout believe pulling these chariots assures them heavenly salvation. The giant raths are unwieldy and almost impossible to turn, and once they get started they are nearly unstoppable. Tens of thousands of ecstatic singing and dancing Hindus crowd in front of the chariots as they make their way through town. There are accounts in centuries past of fanatics throwing

> "one of the most stupendous and fanatical processions anywhere"

themselves under the gigantic wheels in order to die in God's sight. The British, suitably impressed, adopted the word "juggernaut" into the English language.

When You Go:

Non-Hindu visitors cannot enter the temple complex in Puri but can watch the action from nearby rooftops (try the Raghunandan Library, opposite the main gate). You are free to become part of the throng of humanity on the streets below. If you arrive in Puri early, there are some interesting immersion rituals with the three deities in the weeks prior to the Car Festival. The Jagannath chariot pulls are also common sights in other large Indian cities, like Mumbai (Bombay).

Web Coordinate:

www.whatsgoingon. com/100things/carfestival

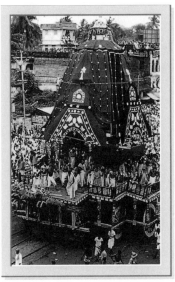

India Tourist Office, New York

173

Holi

Various Locations, Northern and Eastern India

GPS Varies

Holi festival! Holi chaos! Holi mess! Welcome to Holi, India's fluorescent Hindu Mardi Gras where no one is safe from "transcending" into something that resembles a Jackson Pollack canvas! It is the most colorful, friendly battle on Earth.

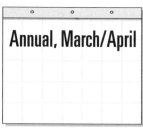

Annual, March/April

Celebrated for the week around the full moon of Phalguna, Holi is a time for shedding inhibitions and ignoring the caste system in celebration of spring and the approaching harvest season. Holi is really about pushing spring fever to full tilt, a celebration meant to demonstrate the triumph of good over evil. Everyone is lighthearted, playful, and ready for some serious mischief. Also known as *Phag* or *Shigma*, the frenzy takes place all across northern and eastern India.

The action begins on the night before the full moon, when huge bonfires are built with the leaves and twigs left over from the winter. To appease the Hindu fire god Hutashani, the locals offer ears of corn, new vegetables, coconuts, butter, and flowers to the fire.

But the next morning is when all hell breaks loose and the "audi-ence participation" segment of the festival really kicks in. Vibrantly colored *gulal* powders are thrown on friends, relatives, and strangers as a symbol of spring. The powders are also mixed with water and dumped off balconies onto the crowds below. It's a free-for-all the likes of which you have probably never witnessed. Soon everyone (and every surface) is covered with the brilliant dyes. In other words, it will definitely be a bad hair day! Throughout the rest of the day there are noisy makeshift parades, feasts, dancing in the streets, and—in true Indian fashion—fireworks galore.

While it is most closely linked with Lord Krishna, "the artistic one who dyes the world with bliss," there are many myths about the ori-

174

gin of Holi. The most popular is the story of Prahlad, a child sent by the gods to deliver the land of Braj from the cruelty of its demonic ruler Hiranyakashap. The king's sister, who was "immune" to fire, offered to take the boy in her lap and sit in a bonfire that would kill him but not her. But because of his virtue (and devotion to the god Vishnu), the child survived unscathed, and Hiranyakashap's sister was torched. Hence, bonfires and offerings are a big part Holi.

> "the most colorful, friendly battle on Earth"

When You Go:

As you can imagine, visitors are a prime target during Holi, so it's a good idea to wear old clothes that you won't mind leaving behind. Be especially careful with your eyes and ears, as the dyes seem to get everywhere. Put your money and wallet in a plastic bag before stepping into the fray. Blondes beware: the dyes are strong and you may look like a New Wave punk long after the anarchy is over.

Web Coordinate:

www.whatsgoingon.com/100things/holi

India Tourist Office, New York

Pushkar Camel Fair

Pushkar, Rajasthan, India

GPS Lat: 26.46666 N Lon: 074.60000 E

No global vagabond's itinerary is complete without a visit to the Pushkar Camel Fair. It is definitely the most chaotic convention of camels you will ever witness. During the week before the full moon of the Hindu month of Karttika, over 200,000 buyers, sellers, and gawkers invade the peaceful, holy

Annual, November

village of Pushkar (where the usual population is only 11,000). It is a caliber of mayhem that can only happen in India—an assault of color, laughter, and energy topped with a healthy dose of spirituality.

You'll find the Camel Fair situated in the desert just to the west of town. The focus is on buying and selling camels; about 30,000 of the snarling beasts trade hands during the week. There is also plenty of camel racing and camel polo. The Rajasthani men and women get all decked out in dazzlingly bright outfits, and young children run around everywhere.

The Camel Fair began as a religious pilgrimage and has grown into a gargantuan spectacle. Consumer product marketing in India means reaching out to over a half-million rural villages like Pushkar, and events like the Camel Fair are prime opportunities for corporations to push their goods and services on a crowd that never knew they needed them. Despite this alarmingly modern intrusion, the Pushkar Camel Fair is still a hypnotic, multipurpose extravaganza with something for everyone.

If you are in the market for a camel, you will have no problem finding one at bargain prices! And since this is a trading fair, there is a wide range of handicrafts, bangles, embroidery, and brassware available for your bartering pleasure. Acrobats, jugglers, snake charmers, mystics, and fire-eaters round out the scene. From morning until night, it's a nonstop photo op.

> "the most chaotic convention of camels"

Pushkar is an important Hindu religious site, with over 400 ninth-century temples scattered around Anasagar Lake. It is one of only a few sites in India with a temple dedicated to Brahman, the Creator. Legend has it that the lake at Pushkar miraculously appeared on the spot where the petal of a lotus blossom fell from the hands of Lord Brahman. Believers flock here to bathe in the holy water and absolve their sins.

When You Go:

Pushkar is a strictly vegetarian and dry town: meat, eggs, milk, and liquor are banned. But there is still some decadence to be had—look out for a notorious, mildly hallucinogenic local beverage, the *bhang lhassi*. Be sure to take plenty of film as you won't find much for sale in Pushkar. Accommodations are tight, but you might consider roughing it in style at the temporary Royal Tent Camp.

Web Coordinate:

www.whatsgoingon.com/100things/pushkar

Dave Freeman

Maha Kumbh Mela

Allahabad, Uttar Pradesh, India

GPS Lat: 25.45000 N Lon: 081.83333 E

The Maha Kumbh Mela practically defies description. Simply put, it is the largest gathering of humanity on Earth. It is also the greatest and holiest of all Hindu festivals, but it happens only once every twelve years. It covers over 3,600 acres and has been celebrated since the second century B.C. At the Maha Kumbh

> **Every twelve years**
> **(2001, 2013, 2025),**
> **March**

Mela in 1989, it is estimated that 18 million pilgrims gathered in Allahabad.

The purpose of the event is for people to bathe in the sacred Ganga, or Ganges, River. Allahabad is where the muddy Ganga and fast-moving Yumana rivers come together, and this meeting point, or *triveni sangram*, is believed to have great soul-cleansing powers. In fact, the *triveni sangram* is considered to be the place where the devout can cross between the material world and Nirvana.

The Maha Kumbh Mela is especially important for India's legions of *sadhus*, or ascetic wanderers. These sages are a fixture in all parts of the country and are easily recognized by their barely clad ash-covered bodies and dreadlocks. Although they are essentially loners, the gathering gives them the chance to reestablish contact with their sects.

Crowds await word from astrologers (India created astrology as we know it) for the most auspicious time to get in the water. Then the rush begins. The first in for their dip are always the legions of elite Naga Sadhus. The police and military are in full force to manage the unmanageable, but the eventual stampede sometimes results in tragedy. Over one hundred pilgrims drowned at the Maha Kumbh Mela in 1989, and accounts say that 18,000 people perished when the event was held in 1759.

Predictably, the Maha Kumbh Mela is founded in myth. It is believed that long ago the gods and demons fought a great battle over a pitcher, or *kumbh*. This pitcher contained the nectar of immortality and came from the bottom of the ocean. As you can guess, the gods eventually defeated the demons and got the chance to drink the nectar. Four drops of the nectar fell to earth during the battle and landed where the cities of Allahabad, Hardiwar, Nasik, and Ujjain are located today.

At three-year intervals between the celebration at Allahabad, other lesser Kumbh Melas occur at the other three cities where the nectar fell. These gatherings are also huge events, but the Maha Kumbh Mela has no rival anywhere for sheer spectacle.

> "the largest gathering of humanity on Earth"

When You Go:

Get there early, as there are hundreds of parades and rituals on the days leading up to the principal immersion. Be generous—clothing, food, and money are given to the *sadhus* and the needy during the event (it might help you in future lives). And read Vikram Seth's novel *A Suitable Boy* for an account of the Maha Kumbh Mela in the early 1950s, when hundreds drowned in the river.

Web Coordinate:

www.whatsgoingon.com/100things/kumbhmela

India Tourist Office, New York

Paro Tsechu

Paro Dzong, Paro, Bhutan

GPS Lat: 27.38333 N Lon: 089.51666 E

Have you ever seen a monk dressed as a monkey man, hooting and hollering and doing a little dance? Every year in Paro, Bhutan, monks dressed as monkeys, bird-men, and other festive creatures do spiritual jigs in the name of Buddhism. It's the biggest and most raucous event in the world's most mysterious country.

Annual, March/April

Bhutan is nearly the same as it was thousands of years ago, and tourists are largely kept out of the country (a limited number are allowed in each year). Leaders are dedicated to keeping the authenticity of ancient Buddhist traditions in a country that is over 90 percent farmers. Bhutan's festivals are held in honor of Guru Rinpoche, the mystic who brought Buddhist teachings to Bhutan from Tibet. They aren't tailored for tourists.

Thousands travel from afar each year for five days of fellowship during Paro Tsechu. They gather in the courtyard of the Paro Dzong, one of hundreds of medieval monasteries that are the architectural pride of Bhutan. Foreign vistors must strictly adhere to Bhutanese customs, such as always walking clockwise around a dzong.

During the Tsechu, traditional Himalayan Buddhist dances teach lessons, confer blessings, and exorcise evils. Lamas and trained laypersons wear masks portraying deities, heroes, demons, and animals. They meditate while leaping and whirling, generating a spiritual power that affects spectators.

In the Dance of the Lord of the Cremation Grounds, a patch of human skin is set down in the middle of the courtyard and four skeleton dancers do an exorcism ritual. *Gings* (celestial beings) run through the audience, beating on drums and even people's heads to drive out evil spirits. Dramatic reenactments of mythical events are interspersed with comedy to lighten up the crowd.

At dawn on the last day of the Tsechu, a *thongdrel,* or very large tapestry depicting Guru Rinpoche, is unrolled and displayed on a wall of the dzong. This is the most important day, since the thongdrel brings enlightenment to all who view it. As soon as the first rays of the sun touch the thongdrel, it is put away for another year.

> "the biggest and most raucous event in the world's most mysterious country"

If you ever start feeling a bit too westernized, head for the simplicity of Bhutan. You'll witness a culture that doesn't exist anymore in other parts of the world—where the people are real, the festivals aren't commercialized, and you still have to walk clockwise around the dzong.

When You Go:

Druk Air is Bhutan's only airline, which flies into Bhutan's only airport, in Paro. Flights are often delayed for days because of weather. Bhutan's not cheap, either. Tourists must spend at least $220 per day. It is extremely difficult to travel alone in the country, so most people use one of the handful of Bhutan-registered travel agents to plan trips. With a tour operator you'll probably stay in decent lodgings, but most accommodations in Bhutan are probably lower in quality than what you're used to.

Web Coordinate:

www.whatsgoingon.com/100things/parotsechu

Marie Brown

181

International Dragon Boat Championships

Shing Mun River, Hong Kong, People's Republic of China

GPS Lat: 22.28333 N Lon: 114.15000 E

At the International Dragon Boat Championships, the fusion of competition and tradition create the most colorful and spirited boat race in the world. The Hong Kong races are the premier championship of traditional dragon boat races, held each year on the fifth day of the fifth lunar month. Associations from all over Asia and around the world—from the Philippines to Norway—travel to Hong Kong's Shing Mun River to sweat it out in the prestigious race.

Dragon boat racing dates back to 278 B.C., when poet Qu Yuan roamed the country, banished from his homeland because of his liberal views. When he learned that his state had been invaded, he put rocks in his sleeves and threw himself into the river. Fishermen raced out to save him in their boats, but they were too late, and they spent the night beating the water with their paddles to prevent his body from being eaten by fish. They threw rice dumplings wrapped in silk into the river to feed his spirit. Rice dumplings are still eaten at dragon boat festivals.

Today, races occur throughout the world to commemorate Qu Yuan and the fishermen. Every year, villages throughout China celebrate the anniversary with a festival and races. In Hong Kong, decorated fishing boats line the racecourse, and fireworks blasting throughout the races contribute to the fast and furious pace of the ancient sporting rivalry.

Dragon boats are colorful, elaborately decorated war canoes with carvings of dragon heads and tails on the bows and sterns, respectively. Boats are 30 to 100 feet long and less than 4 feet wide. Anywhere from twenty to one hundred rowers propel the boats. Teams

also include a helmsperson and gong players and drummers, who sit in the middle and back of the boats and set the pace of the rowing. Some modern-day dragon boat teams include a member who stands upright in the boat, waving his arms and scanning the water for Qu Yuan's body.

Dragon boat paddlers dip their oars only a few inches into the water and row at a rapid rate, causing the boat to glide quickly across the water. Boats travel 500 meters (1,640 feet) in about two and a half minutes! Races are often rowdy, but it's a good thing that some early practices are extinct. In years past, spectators threw stones at unpopular boats. And it used to be considered good luck if a boat capsized and at least one person drowned.

When You Go:

Hong Kong is highly developed and tourism-savvy, so conditions are on par with other major cities. Take some money for the super shopping scene and high hotel rates—June is in the peak season for travel. Pack clothes with extreme heat and humidity in mind. Before you explore, climb up to Victoria Peak for a spectacular view of the city; it's a great way to get your bearings.

> "the most colorful and spirited boat race in the world"

Web Coordinate:

www.whatsgoingon.com/100things/dragonboat

Hounen Matsuri
(Tagata Fertility Festival)

Tagata Jinja Shrine, Komaki, Aichi Prefecture, Japan

GPS Lat: 35.28333 N Lon: 136.91666 E

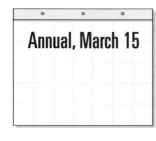

Every year on March 15, Japan pulls out its biggest penis and parades it around for everyone to see. It's a part of Hounen Matsuri, locally called the Penis Festival, arguably the most exposed fertility festival in the world. The fun is centered

Annual, March 15

around an 8-foot, 1,000-pound wooden penis! Tens of thousands of people flock to the little town to get a glimpse of the phallus-centered festivities that started over 1,500 years ago as a Shinto religious offering to ensure fertility. Not only will you get an eyeful of the town's huge wooden penis, but, if you're so inclined, you can eat penis candy, touch penis figures for good luck, and drink lots of free sake. But don't worry—this festival isn't about sex, just penises.

The huge wooden penis that is *the* penis of the Penis Festival is carved out of a Japanese cypress tree trunk. Each year the old penis is replaced with a new one. It resides on a shrine that is carried by three groups of twenty men, all forty-two years old (an age that needs special spiritual care, according to ancient beliefs). They walk, run, stop abruptly, and speed around in circles with the massive shrine.

The year-round home to the giant penis and many more phalluses is Komaki's Tagata Jinja Shrine. Stone penises decorate the shrine's gardens, and the walls of the shrine are lined with all types of erect penises. Even the shrine's bell is penis-shaped.

The big day is jam-packed with fun-loving participants of all types—children and elderly, women and men, native Japanese and tourists. Says one-time Aichi resident Ivan Small, "You can buy little penis charms, little statues where you pull up the barrel and a penis pops out, cakes in the shapes of penises, penis lollipops. It's a very

184

pop-culture thing. People go there not necessarily because they want to be fertile, but because they think it's funny."

In the procession are priests, musicians, and other special characters. A group of women embrace special wooden phalluses wrapped in red paper, and as they pass, spectators touch the tips to ensure good health for their children. Sake is passed out along the route. The main penis is carried through the "legs" of the shrine's *torii* (bird) gate and installed in the temple's main showroom, where it stands at attention for the rest of the year to promote penis worship (and envy) for all comers.

> "the most exposed fertility festival in the world"

When You Go:

Komaki is just north of Nagoya between Tokyo and Osaka. You'll probably have better luck finding a hotel in the larger city of Nagoya. The Tagata Jinja Shrine is at Tagata-cho 152. Parking is tight, so take a train. If you've got the time, stick around for the Vagina Festival that happens in Komaki within a week of the Penis Festival. (Now that's equal opportunity!)

Web Coordinate:

www.whatsgoingon.com/100things/tagata

The Chubu Weekly, Nagoya, Japan

Sanja Matsuri

Asakusa, Tokyo, Japan

GPS Lat: 35.75000 N Lon: 139.50000 E

The Sanja Matsuri is the biggest, baddest, most boisterous Buddhist festival in all of Japan. This huge parade draws over 2 million people into the streets of Tokyo's district of Asakusa.

Annual, May
(third weekend)

The festival is centered around *mikoshi*, the elaborately decorated shrines that weigh over 500 pounds and are carried by teams of locals. Mikoshi house local deities who leave their shrines once a year to visit the community and bestow their blessings for the coming year. Carrying a shrine is a great honor, and shrine-bearers entertain the god within by being wild and carrying the shrine in zig zags, pushing it up and down, swaying, and running with it in all directions. This also shows that they are valorous. During Sanja Matsuri, one hundred mikoshi are paraded in the streets, and since the streets are extremely crowded, they move very slowly.

The parades of mikoshi are led by musicians who clap out a steady rhythm on wooden blocks, play drums, and blow whistles while the shrine-bearers shout. The streets of Tokyo are the most lively during Sanja Matsuri, wall-to-wall with people from all over Japan. You'll see geishas, musicians, dancers, children, and even dogs wearing traditional coats!

During this time, Tokyo's *yakuza* crime gangs openly display their body tattoos, something usually against the law. Though it's technically forbidden, many gang members strip down to loincloth-like underwear and jump on the shrines to show off.

In the precincts of the temple, priests perform special ceremonies and locals play music created especially for Sanja Matsuri. Elaborately costumed dancers perform the beautiful ancient Edo (the historical name of Tokyo) dance called *binzasara no mai*. The dancers play the unique binzasara (a snake-like instrument made of slats of wood that makes a clacking rhythm), the *shiteti* (a circular hand drum), and flutes while performing the lion and seed-scattering dances.

Sanja Matsuri is held by the Sensoji Shrine, the primary and oldest Buddhist temple in Tokyo. This temple is dedicated to two fishermen and a village elder who in the seventh century found a statue of the goddess Kannon in the river. *Sanja* means "three noble men."

Don't miss your chance to see Tokyo at its liveliest. Brave the crowds of people for a few days to experience a truly Japanese-style party. It will please the deities, and you might have some fun in the process!

When You Go:

Stop by the Asakusa Tourist Center to get a map of the parade route and other tourist goodies. If you're being cautious, keep a distance from the mikoshi. But don't watch from a location that's higher than the parade—it's considered rude and a slight to the deities. The streets are packed with people (who push and shove you out of the way), so head to the Sensoji Temple for the best view of Sanja Matsuri ceremonies.

> "the biggest, baddest, most boisterous Buddhist festival"

Web Coordinate:

www.whatsgoingon.com/100things/sanja

Sapporo Snow Festival (Yuki Matsuri)

Sapporo, Hokkaido, Japan

GPS Lat: 43.08333 N Lon: 141.35000 E

Don't let those February blues get you down—carve some snow! That's what a few students of Sapporo, Japan, did in 1950. Their idea to beat the winter doldrums has evolved into a spectacular winter display, internationally known for its massive recreations of famous buildings from around the world.

**Annual,
February 5-11**

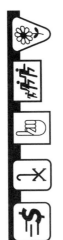

Sapporo's huge Snow Festival, called Yuki Matsuri, draws over 2 million people to the temporary winter wonderland. For seven days, Odori Park and the Makomanai and Suskino districts host over 300 snow and ice sculptures depicting cartoon characters, detailed artistic reliefs, fantasy characters, architectural pieces, and local personalities. An International Snow Statues Contest attracts sculpting teams from all over the world, including snowless places like Hawaii and Southeast Asia.

The main attraction of the festival is a nearly life-size recreation of a famous building such as St. Paul's Cathedral in London or Salzburg's Dom Cathedral. They've even created a fantastical depiction of aliens visiting the most interesting attractions on the planet (e.g., Egyptian pyramids, the Taj Mahal, and the Great Wall of China). The multistory sculptures have very detailed interiors, and bundled-up visitors are allowed to explore the insides of these buildings as well as the outsides. At night, colored lights illuminate the insides and outsides of the sculptures.

Several smaller sculptures at the Snow Festival follow the same theme of the main one. One year, Odori Park turned into "France Square," with a replica of the Church of the Dome of the Hotel des Invalides in Paris. Near the replica were a snow sculpture recreating the Statue of Napoleon and a relief of the Mona Lisa. For the three sculptures, 546 5-ton trucks of snow and 4,660 sculptors were used over twenty-eight days of carving!

Creating such massive works requires not only the energy of a lot of people, but also their dedication, since time and weather eventually destroy these masterpieces. A considerable amount of the work is done by the military—the Ground Self-Defense Force of Sapporo. Large frames are packed with snow, and once the snow hardens, sculptors work by night—sunlight softens and endangers sculptures during carving. In addition to these official efforts, hundreds of Sapporo citizens get involved and carve their own sculptures. Some even have snow slides for children!

Come out of your February hibernation for a few days and head to Sapporo. There, the friendly people will warm up your winter by offering you a glimpse of their transiently beautiful creations.

> "a spectacular winter display, internationally known for its massive recreations of famous buildings"

When You Go:

February temperatures in Sapporo are below zero and sidewalks are slippery, so bundle up and wear suitable shoes. Since the festival is free, you'll have money for souvenirs. Climb the TV tower at Odori Park, where you can get a great view of the sculptures and of Sapporo. And Sapporo is known for its great nightlife scene, so peripheral events such as concerts, dancing, and fireworks shows are lots of fun.

Web Coordinate:

www.whatsgoingon.com/100things/snowfest

Japan Information Center, NY

Shuni-e (Omizutori)

Todai-ji Temple, Nigatsu-do Hall, Nara, Japan

GPS Lat: 34.68333 N Lon: 135.83333 E

You may think that fire and water don't mix, but each March in Nara, Japan, monks of Todai-ji Temple present the people with the holiest of holy waters and a shower of burning embers during Shuni-e, a furious and fiery religious rite.

Annual, March 1-14

Without Shuni-e, the "Ceremony of the Second Month," spring supposedly will not come. For fourteen days, monks pray for world peace and repent the world's sins. Shuni-e is popularly called Omizutori, or "Water Drawing Festival," after its most spectacular rite, which has been celebrated every year for about 1,250 years.

For eleven days before Omizutori, monks engage in religious ceremonies, like the Rite of Exorcism and torch-bearing processions. On the twelfth night, a monk kills the fire in the "eternal lamp," lit at last year's ceremony, and lights a new one using flint and steel.

In 752, a monk named Jitchu saw the gods practicing a beautiful ceremony of repentance. Jitchu brought it to the human world, but one day in Heaven equals 400 human years, so Jitchu decided to perform the ceremony at high speed. This ceremony is called Hashiri no Gyoho, the Ritual of Circumambulation, when monks try to catch up to the time of Buddha's world. Carrying torches, eleven monks march around Nigatsu-do. They chant, while others blow conch shells, shake rattles, and wave swords to ward off evil spirits. Other monks hidden under a veil pray for repentance, their huge shadows glimmering on the wall behind them. The marching monks increase their speed until they are running around the altar as fast as they can, and the praying monks quicken their ritual. Suddenly, the veil is dropped, the praying monks are revealed, and the torch-bearing monks swing their torches, showering embers onto the crowd. Believe it or not, the spectators don't run away from the fire. They try to catch the embers as good luck charms!

At 2 A.M., monks draw water from a sacred well. A few drops supposedly will bring healing or will stall the aging process. Once a year, water from the well is given to the people. It is also poured into a pot filled with water taken in all of the more than 1,200 past rituals!

Todai-ji Temple is famous for this strict religious exercise and also because it's the largest wooden building in the world. But it has burned down twice. Maybe next time someone will think of putting out the holy fire with the holy water!

When You Go:

Various hotels and traditional Japanese inns are available in Nara, which is most easily reached via a one-hour express train ride from Osaka. A great place for a picnic in Nara is Sarusawa Pond, attached to a fish and animal sanctuary. You will also be able to watch the cherry trees bloom, which usually happens shortly after the ceremony is over, in the middle to end of March.

Web Coordinate:

www.whatsgoingon.com/100things/shunie

Japan Information Center, NY

Naadam

Ulaanbaatar, Mongolia

GPS Lat: 47.90000 N Lon: 106.86666 E

At the Naadam Festival, you're in for a treat—Mongolian style. Stock up on dried curds and fermented mare's milk, pack up your *ger*, and tie on a *dahl*, because you're going to the biggest Mongolian celebration of the year! Occurring in the nation's capital, Ulaanbaatar, the festival offers a disorderly dis-

Annual, July 11-13

play of wrestling, archery, and horseracing. These events are known as the Three Main Games of Men. Mongolian citizens travel from afar to watch the traditional sports and enjoy the accompanying Mongolian foods, crafts, and folk dancing.

Mongolia's own special style of wrestling (similar to sumo) is over 7,000 years old and is the country's most popular sport. Wrestlers dress in skin-tight "Speedos" and open vests to prove that they are really men. (Once a popular champion was discovered to be a woman, causing much embarrassment!) There are no weight categories or age limits; the wrestler's goal is to get his opponent to lose his balance, and the first man to touch the ground with his elbow or knee loses. The loser must walk under the raised arms of the winner as a sign of respect. Then the victor dances around a flag in the center of the field.

Both men and women participate in archery, the second of the Three Main Games. Using a compound bow, archers aim for rows of woven leather rings, several meters across. The openings of the rings face upward, which makes it harder to score points.

The third of the Three Main Games of Men doesn't have much to do with men at all. In the horse races of Naadam, children ages three to twelve ride as far as 17 miles! The little ones—actually excellent riders—face a challenging course of rivers, ravines, and hills. Still, it is ultimately a horse race. If the rider falls off the horse and it crosses the line first, the horse still wins the race.

The winning horse receives the title "Forehead of Ten Thousand Race Horses." The winning rider and four runners-up each receive a bowl of *airag* (fermented mare's milk). Each rider drinks some of the milk and pours some on the horse's rear end. A herald loudly chants verses espousing the virtues of the horse, its rider, and its owner. Then it's time to wipe the Forehead's rump and call it a day.

> "a disorderly display of wrestling, archery, and horseracing"

When You Go:

Getting to Mongolia is tough, but it could be worse—thankfully, Ulaanbaatar is Mongolia's capital. Airlines aren't particularly reliable, so take the TransMongolian Railways from Beijing or Moscow. Hotels are available in Ulaanbaatar, but they're not particularly comfy and are usually full during the festivities, so why not sleep as the locals do? Many camp year-round in *ger*s, felt tents that can be rolled up and carried. And if you really feel the spirit, dress traditionally in the local *dahl* cloth.

Web Coordinate:

www.whatsgoingon.com/100things/naadam

Pat Lanza/Boojum Expeditions

Bisket Jaatra

Bhaktapur (Bhadgoan), Nepal

GPS Lat: 27.68333 N Lon: 085.41666 E

Forget the tuxedo, champagne, and silly hats—because Bisket Jaatra is a New Year's celebration that doesn't conform to typical stereotypes. The four days of parades, bizarre rituals, merriment, and chaos really wake up the usually sleepy, ancient city of Bhaktapur. Bisket Jaatra begins on the first day of the Nepalese

Annual, April/May

solar calendar and signals the coming of spring and the banishing of demons. (*Bisket* roughly translates to "snake slaughter.")

The action begins with a maddening procession, featuring a huge three-tiered chariot, that begins at the Bhairab Temple and lumbers through the tiny, cobbled streets of Bhaktapur. Inside the chariot are the trappings of the omnipotent guardian deity, Lord Bhairab, who represents the destructive force of Shiva. Bhairab's shining brass mask is usually locked up in the temple but is allowed to leave one day each year to go for a ride. Riding along with the mask is a mysterious locked box that the faithful believe contains the severed head of Bhairab, a deity who materialized as a human a millennium or so ago.

The procession ends in a tug-of-war with the chariot. The men from the southern part of town pull against the men from the northern neighborhoods in a struggle for good fortune in the coming year. The mayhem continues for the next three days with more parades, torch-lit street dances, and the offering of rice, marigold garlands, red tikka powder, and candles at the dozens of temples that dot the town.

On the final day of the festival, chariots are pulled into a clearing on the south end of town where the *lingam* is raised. The lingam is a ceremonial 80-foot tree trunk with a crossbeam, roughly carved to resemble a phallus.

Townspeople watch intently as the mammoth lingam is hoisted with ropes into an upright position. This somewhat comical process can take hours, and sometimes the lingam comes crashing down, injuring—or even killing—people. Sometimes the operation is a total failure (a bad omen that may bring disaster to the nation). If and when the lingam is erect, the crowds cheer as two long banners representing evil snake demons unfurl to the ground. At the end of the day, the lingam is toppled down and the new year officially begins.

When You Go:

There are few places to stay in Bhaktapur, so bunking in Kathmandu is probably your best bet. Bhaktapur is about 6.5 miles due east of Kathmandu and makes for a great bike ride through rice paddies and small villages (beat-up one-speeds can be rented everywhere). For a panoramic view of the Bisket Jaatra mayhem, consider parking yourself on the balcony of the Cafe Nyatapola near the Taumadhi Tol square.

> "four days of parades, bizarre rituals, merriment, and chaos"

Web Coordinate:

www.whatsgoingon.com/100things/bisketjaatra

Dave Freeman

Ati-Atihan

Kalibo, Island of Panay, Philippines

GPS Lat: 11.70000 N Lon: 122.33333 E

"*Hala bira, puera pasma!*" screams an ape who is dancing with a nun. "*Hala bira, puera pasma!*" replies an astronaut who then takes a swig of fermented coconut wine and passes it to the clown he has his arm around.

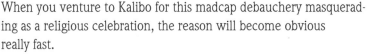

**Annual,
January 16-19**

This communal Ati-Atihan mantra translates to "Keep on going, no tiring." When you venture to Kalibo for this madcap debauchery masquerading as a religious celebration, the reason will become obvious really fast.

This uniquely Philippine fiesta, often compared to Mardi Gras, is always celebrated the second week after Epiphany (January 6). For the last three days of this week-long festival, the entire town erupts with dancing, costumed revelers covered in red, blue, and white chalk and soot.

Visitors who wander into the boisterous routine of drums-and-whistles, stampers-and-chanters, and dancing-in-the-street mayhem are welcomed like old friends. Some islanders may paint you in soot and feed you a meal of *lechon* (roasted pig).

Ati-Atihan's raucousness dates back to A.D. 1210, when Negrito aborigines known as *Atis* were the sole inhabitants of the Panay Islands. During this time, down in Borneo, ten Datu families and their followers fled northward to escape oppression. They came to Panay, and in a brilliant real estate venture, they bought some of the Atis' turf for only a golden *salakot* (wide-brimmed hat), a *kris* (wavy-edged battle sword), and a long golden necklace. To celebrate the closing of the deal, the refugees hosted a feast for their new neighbors. They sounded gongs, had too much to drink, and to symbolize the pact, smeared their faces and bodies with soot, affectionately imitating the Negritos.

The Panay settlers lived in fear of slave-hunting pirates from Mindanao. After a failed raid of the island, a couple of Spanish friars convinced the islanders that the baby Jesus (Santo Niño) had driven off the attackers. Today's festival incorporates the ritual of *patapak*, during which revelers can be seen with the effigy of the holy child on their shoulders shouting, "*Viva el Señor Santo Niño!*"—Long live the child Jesus!

Ati-Atihan's popularity has inspired many similar celebrations in the Philippines' Western Visayas region this time of year, but Kalibo's is the oldest, most authentic, and best loved national riot, er, holiday.

Philippine Department of Tourism

When You Go:

During Ati-Atihan, many visitors pitch tents or just roll out a sleeping bag on the beach. The Philippine Department of Tourism can help you get accommodations with a family in Kalibo for a modest price. The best hotels for Ati-Atihan are the ones that overlook the Kalibo's main plaza, ground zero for much of the bedlam. Hotel prices increase tenfold during the festival, running you about P450–500 (still only about $12).

"madcap debauchery masquerading as a religious celebration"

Web Coordinate:

www.whatsgoingnon.com/100things/atiatihan

Chung Yuan Ghost Month Festival

Chu Pu Tan Temple, Keelung, Taiwan

GPS Lat: 25.16666 N Lon: 121.36666 E

During late summer in Taiwan, a feeling of caution envelopes the country. It's a fearful time when the gates of the netherworld open for an entire month. Swimming pools, beaches, and roads are almost empty, and few people venture outdoors after sundown. Weddings are postponed, important business deals

Annual, August/September

shelved. Millions of souls are back on Earth, and they want to be feasted, entertained, prayed to and paid off, and they try to take revenge on the unwary. One of the most auspicious days to appease dead souls during this period is the Chung Yuan Festival.

During "Ghost Month" in Taiwan and other parts of Asia, the deceased come back and demand attention and care. Families set out food and incense for dead relatives, along with fake money for them to use in the underworld. But the biggest fuss is over "hungry ghosts" or "lonely ghosts," souls with no living descendants, who can be ill-tempered or destructive during their vacation on Earth. It's a real-life version of *The Night of the Living Dead*!

On the day of the Chung Yuan Festival, banquet tables set out at temples overflow with offerings of meat, fish, vegetables, canned food, and alcoholic beverages. Hogs are sacrificed and roasted on spits, and Taiwanese operas are performed nonstop to entertain the ghosts while they dine. After the banquet, the temples are filled with *tou teng*, containers of rice topped with symbolic evil-dispelling objects like knives, umbrellas, and mirrors.

The massive Chu Pu Tan Temple in the northern town of Keelung is a popular place to witness Chung Yuan. An impressive procession makes its way from the temple to the seaside, with floats, bands, and house-shaped lanterns. The celebration culminates when the lanterns are set on fire and put out to sea.

The origins of Ghost Month remain a mystery. Taoists believe it honors the birthday of Yenlo Wang, the Demon King. Buddhists believe a legend about a man named Mu Lan who traveled to the netherworld to visit his recently deceased mother. She had been evil and selfish on Earth. When Mu Lan tried to feed her, the food morphed into ashes every time it touched her lips. When he returned to Earth, Mu Lan asked his Buddhist master if his mother could be saved. The monk replied that she could achieve salvation only if Mu Lan prepared food and drink offerings for all lost souls and if all monks and nuns chanted and prayed for her. Talk about one dysfunctional family affecting everyone!

> "a fearful time when the gates of the netherworld open"

When You Go:

Look out for ghosts—they can take on human form at will during Ghost Month. You can spot ghosts by looking at people's feet; feet of Taiwanese ghosts never touch the ground. The port city of Keelung is forty-five minutes north of Taipei. While there, check out the huge open-air Miaokou market and visit the nearby Northeast Coast National Scenic Area with its awe-inspiring Henry Moore-esque cliffs and rock formations. When you pack, remember that this is typhoon season and you may get wet.

Web Coordinate:

www.whatsgoingon.com/100things/ghost

Taiwan Visitors Association

Ngan Kin Jeh (Chinese Vegetarian Festival)

Phuket, Thailand

GPS Lat: 07.86666 N Lon: 098.36666 E

Annual, October
(ten days)

At Thailand's Chinese Vegetarian Festival, no one eats meat—the skewered, sliced, and tenderized flesh is all 100 percent pure, Grade A human. That's right, at the Ngan Kin Jeh in Phuket, Thailand, devout Buddhists perform the most stomach-churning religious ceremony in the world. "Ascetic" rituals include cheek-piercing using six-foot rods, self-flagellation with axes, and climbing a ladder of razor blades.

In the middle of the last century, a traveling opera company from China responded to a mysterious fever by going that extra masochistic mile to appease the gods. It worked. Thus began the annual mutilation festival now held in coincidence with Taoist Lent. Anything goes—and the more gruesome, the better.

To prepare, volunteer "Warriors of the Gods" abstain from meat, alcohol, cigarettes, sex, lying, quarrelling, and killing. Then, by performing disgusting ascetic feats, the warriors are possessed by the Nine Emperor Gods. Priests use hooks, branches, steel rods, plastic poles, and glass skewers to pierce the cheeks of warriors and insert instruments of torture. Instruments may include umbrellas, saw blades, and chains or poles. In some cases, poles connect several warriors, sort of like a string of carp.

Torture instrument affixed, the warrior goes into a trance, shaking and shouting, whooping and hopping. With sixty or more warriors possessed by the Nine Emperor Gods, the temple yard can be quite a zoo! No one bleeds much, and no one seems to feel pain. Believers say that's proof that the gods are at work.

With the Warrior-kabobs, everyone parades through town, and more people inflict pain on themselves in creative ways. There are

"the most stomach-churning religious ceremony in the world

self-flaggelators, blade-lickers, piercers, and hot-coal runners. Young men carrying altars through the street get burned by firecrackers hurled at the altars to cleanse them of evil spirits. (These aren't regular firecrackers—some are made of thousands of little sticks of dynamite.) In the evening, hundreds of young men climb the 40-foot Bladed Ladder, which sports seventy-two razor-sharp rungs.

At the end of an exhausting day of self-torture, Warriors of the Gods visit an old priest who de-possesses them. After some banging and chanting, they open their eyes and walk away as if nothing happened. If that's not a good party trick, what is?

When You Go:

Before you go, load up on the vaccinations: malaria, Hepatitis A and B, Japanese encephalitis, rabies, and typhoid. Be extra careful during the festival: AIDS and HIV are rampant in Thailand, and safety doesn't seem to be a top priority at this festival. Watch out for pickpockets and scam artists who prey on tourists—just use common sense. Phuket is accustomed to westerners, but it's still a good idea to treat everyone with respect and dress modestly.

Web Coordinate:

www.whatsgoingon.com/100things/ngankinjeh

Chaiyos Pinpradab

Tet Nguyen Dan

Ho Chi Minh City, Vietnam

GPS Lat: 10.75000 N Lon: 106.66666 E

Dick Clark has never seen a New Year's celebration like this! Tet Nguyen Dan is the most important and highest-decibel holiday in Vietnam, because the locals believe that the first day (well, first few days) of the new year determines their fortune for the rest of the year.

Annual, January/February

On Tet Nguyen Dan, the locals do everything under their control to make sure that their next year is a happy one: families reunite, deadbeats pay off their debts, everyone avoids arguments, families paint and clean their houses, and it seems like everyone gets a haircut and new clothes. In addition to celebrating the new year, all Vietnamese celebrate their birthdays during Tet—everyone turns a year older on the same day.

The celebration actually starts with a pre-Tet ceremony called Le Tao Quan. This is the day when families make offerings to the Spirit of the Kitchen before he goes to report the family's activities to the mythical Jade Emperor. Families decorate their homes with peach and plum tree blossoms and construct a shrine to ward off evil spirits while the Kitchen God is away. A sacrifice is also offered to all dead family members, who are invited to join the family for the celebration.

During a ritual called Giao Thua, the old year is ushered out and the new year is welcomed. Although gongs and drums have recently replaced firecrackers as the noisemakers of choice, it's still a loud occasion. There's lots of well-wishing for everyone during the celebration—special two-sentence poems are recited, and special trees are planted. Children are given *Li Xi* (lucky money) in red envelopes. The color red brings luck, and paper money brings prosperity.

The first visitor of the year (literally, the first person who sets foot on the grounds of the house) is considered very important. Families

Associated Press/Peter Lennihan

take special care in selecting this visitor—they choose the person they consider the happiest, wealthiest, and most influential they know.

What would a celebration be without special foods? Be sure to sample the most symbolic food eaten during this time, *Banh Chung*. Symbolizing the people of Vietnam and the land on which they toil, Banh Chung is a square, salty, sticky rice cake filled with pork and mung beans that is wrapped in a banana leaf and tied with bamboo string. Yum!

When You Go:

Make your airline reservations early for Tet, as international flights are booked solid with Vietnamese expatriots making the trip. Prepare for limited services when you get there; local businesses (including shops and restaurants) often shut down for a week or more before the holiday. A visa is required for all foreign nationals visiting Vietnam. While no vaccinations are required for entry into Vietnam, typhoid and hepatitis inoculations are strongly recommended.

> "the most important and highest-decibel holiday in Vietnam"

Web Coordinate:

www.whatsgoingon.com/100things/tet

Australia and the Pacific

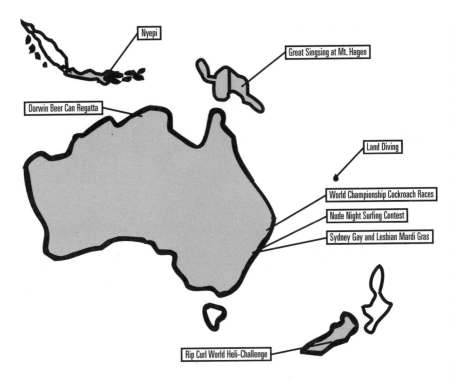

Nyepi

Great Singsing at Mt. Hagen

Darwin Beer Can Regatta

Land Diving

World Championship Cockroach Races

Nude Night Surfing Contest

Sydney Gay and Lesbian Mardi Gras

Rip Curl World Heli-Challenge

Sydney Fringe Festival Nude Night Surfing

Bondi Beach, Sydney, New South Wales, Australia

GPS Lat: 33.91666 S Lon: 151.16666 E

Annual, mid-January

"Nude surfing is a very, very funny thing to do," exclaims Andrew Farrell. And he should know: This self-proclaimed "surf maniac" has participated in Sydney Fringe Festival Nude Night Surfing for the past several years. That's right, nude surfing. It could be the most outrageous expression of freedom and exhibitionism ever created.

Every January, Sydney Fringe Festival Nude Night Surfing contestants flap, bounce, and jiggle their bare essentials in the wind—until they reach the chilly Pacific surf, where things shrivel, shrink, and get all goose-bumpy. But competition is stiff, so to speak: First prize is two nights at a nudist resort.

Thousands of revved-up spectators join a small army of tabloid photographers in extensive yelling and cheering when dozens of brave buck-naked souls attempt to catch the perfect tube. If you plan to participate, you better be looking your best; footage of last year's contest was broadcast in thirty-eight countries. Male contestants outnumber the ladies about four-to-one, but everyone is invited to show their goods (and surfing skills).

The difficult task of judging is done by a panel of surfing and entertainment celebrities. The contest rules demand all participants be "ordinary humans . . . no professional nudists." The action takes place at Sydney's notorious Bondi Beach, a laid-back resort community that is home to local and international "surfies" who flock here year-round for the famous waves.

"What about the surfing?" you ask. Well, let's just say the emphasis is not just on hanging ten, nor on board maneuvering skill. Judging for this "expression session" is based on surfing skill and the ability to entertain. You may be wondering how the experts prepare for competitive nude surfing. "Have no shame, have a good tan and no unsightly blemishes on your behind," notes Farrell.

Spectators at Bondi are a mix of "slinky foxy babes with pierced belly buttons, bemused Japanese tourists, rock stars, foul-mouthed Cockney tabloid photographers looking for a front-page boob-shot, poseurs, lost families, and feral young grommets," according to Farrell. "And the nude surfing spectator is pretty savvy these days," he adds. "They can smell fear in a competitor, sensing if the rider fails to glide close to shore standing proud and erect without a hint of embarrassment." So shed those clothes and prepare to shred!

> "the most outrageous expression of freedom and exhibitionism"

When You Go:

The Nude Night Surfing contest is part of the beloved Sydney Fringe Festival, which takes place every January. This hip alternative to the more stuffy Sydney Festival offers everything from dance and music to theater and an independent film festival. And no, none of the other festival events is held in the nude. After the contest, there's usually a "fully clothed" after-party at the nearby Fringe Festival Club at Bondi Pavilion, on Bondi Beach, featuring the Nude Night Surfing Award Presentation and special guest bands.

Web Coordinate:

www.whatsgoingon.com/100things/nudesurf

Sydney Fringe Festival

Sydney Gay and Lesbian Mardi Gras

Sydney, New South Wales, Australia

GPS Lat: 33.91666 S Lon: 151.16666 E

Annual, February

No matter what your sexual preference, you can't miss the most diverse and passionate display of gay and lesbian pride in the world. Forget the beads, leis, drunken students, and crowded streets typically associated with Mardi Gras. Instead, at the Sydney Gay and Lesbian Mardi Gras, you'll be up to your nose in boas, leather, glitter, g-strings, rubber, saran wrap, erotic acts, visual art, sports, and spectacle. Mardi Gras events go on during the entire month of February, and the fun ends with a huge parade and party.

What began as a clash between gay activists and cops has evolved into Australia's largest tourist attraction. Since it began in 1978, the Mardi Gras has remained an organic organization that grows and changes with the times. "I know for many the joy of Mardi Gras is the pride we have in showing off the strength and creativity of our local community," notes former Mardi Gras president David Mclachlan.

Each year the program for Mardi Gras becomes bigger and more diverse. You'll find a bevy of exhibits, performances, concerts, panels, and events that all examine different aspects of gay and lesbian culture. Recent standouts have included such outrageous offerings as the "Wet Girls Beach Day Picnic," an art exhibit entitled "The Ten Cubicle Suckatorium," and a performance called "Car Maintenance, Explosives and Love."

The official Mardi Gras Parade finale is a rambunctious display of humor, elegance, outrage, and satire. The biggest spectacle in Australia marches through the streets of Sydney, with over 6,000 participants and 700,000 spectators. The parade is really a fun-for-the-whole-family affair and is broadcast on local television.

> "the most diverse and passionate display of gay and lesbian pride"

Pre-parade entertainment (known as "fore-play") includes cheerleaders, drag races, and a crowd favorite—Dykes on Bikes. After the parade, the official Mardi Gras Party takes place nearby at several convention-sized halls at the Old Showgrounds Moore Park.

This big bash attracts over 20,000 revelers, and admittance is restricted to members of the Sydney Gay and Lesbian Mardi Gras organization and their guests. In addition to numerous themed rooms and a small army of disk jockeys, there is always a special, surprise performance. Past appearances have included such gay icons as Boy George, Kylie Minogue, and Thelma Houston.

Some say that Sydney has L.A.'s weather, San Francisco's looks, London's sophistication, and New York's nightlife. What better place for this outrageous, stylish, utlra-queer Mardi Gras?

When You Go:

Plan ahead for this one, as flights to Sydney and hotel rooms are booked months in advance. If you want to watch the parade in style, you can reserve a spot at the grandstand seating on Driver Avenue. The grandstands come complete with a full bar and parade commentary from community celebrities. If you are watching your cash, do what the locals do and watch the spectacle from Moore Park.

Web Coordinate:

www.whatsgoingon.com/100things/gaymardigras

Australian Tourist Commission

Darwin Beer Can Regatta

Mindil Beach, Darwin, Northern Territory, Australia

GPS Lat: 12.38333 S Lon: 130.73333 E

Annual, August

If you're looking for an event representing the evolution of man, then look elsewhere. Darwinians take primal urges very seriously! Every year in early August, Mindil Beach in Darwin, Australia, hosts the Beer Can Regatta, the most outrageous and creative boat race on earth. This local charity event brings together great engineers and great drinkers. Whatever it is that floats your boat, the Darwin Beer Can Regatta has it—in abundance.

Darwin is home to some of Australia's most unique inhabitants and prides itself on being the beer-drinking capital of the world. Darwinians consume an average of 230 liters of "the amber" each year. So it is not surprising that local pastimes revolve around the stuff!

Participants construct everything from life-size beer-can canoes to beer-can Viking warships (complete with fire hoses) during this off-the-wall regatta. Some Darwinians see their boats as a real means of transport. One group sailed their beer-can craft all the way to Singapore. A sure-fire way to offend is by constructing your boat from full beer cans. Other contestants will cry foul, and you'll look like a wuss for not having been able to drink the beer.

You don't have to participate in the regatta to enjoy the melee. Pick up a few of the world's largest bottles of beer, Darwin Stubbies (2.25 liters or 75 ounces), and cheer on the Regatta's twenty or more aluminum masterpieces. Then watch as these craft projects teeter, totter, and probably sink. And remember, you don't have to be a Regatta contestant to have fun. Competitions for landlubbers can be even more wild than any beer-can construction.

Henley-on-Mindil features beach racing in bottomless boats, while scantily clad beauties strut their stuff during the bathing beauty contests. There is also thong-throwing for those who want to practice their pitching technique.

Sideshows are another great part of the fun that surrounds the Beer Can Regatta. Don't miss Rage in the Cage and the Gong Show. Be forewarned—anything goes during the Gong Show. All sorts of misfits get up on stage to exhibit their unique talents. Luckily for them, the stage is protected by a chicken-wire net. Why? Well, sometimes when the audience has had enough, they feel compelled to pelt performers with open bottles of beer.

> "the most outrageous and creative boat race on earth"

When You Go:

Sunscreen and a high tolerance for alcohol are a must. Don't leave home without them. Cheap accommodations can be found in the area around the bus station, but even cheaper ones can be found on the beach itself. After a full day of beer-drinking and thong-throwing, plop yourself onto the sand, relax, and fall asleep. You've earned it!

Web Coordinate:

www.whatsgoingon.com/100things/beercan

Australian Tourist Commission

World Championship Cockroach Races

Brisbane, Queensland, Australia

GPS Lat: 27.50000 S Lon: 153.00000 E

**Annual, January 26
(Australia Day)**

Leave it to the Australians to think up the World Championship Cockroach Races as part of their annual Australia Day festivities. Each year, dozens of tiny, germ-infested roaches face off, all yearning to be champ, and all incited to great levels of competitive fervor by the crowd's screaming and shouting.

What has been called "the greatest gathering of thoroughbred cockroaches in the known universe" began in 1982 when a couple of barflies each claimed that the roaches from his part of town were the fastest in Brisbane. They tested their testosterone- and alcohol-fueled convictions in a parking garage. Thus were these storied races born!

Each year, there are about seven cockroach racing events, including the sprint, the steeplechase, and the main event, the Story Bridge Hotel "Gold Cup." The roach rivals are placed under a can in the middle of a 6-meter ring. Once the can is raised, the first roach to cross the edge of the ring wins.

Anyone can get involved and sponsor a roach racer. Just find a cockroach, give it a fun name, and pay a $5 (Australian) entry fee. If you can't find a strong-looking roach, you can buy one at the contest! Let's hope your filth-monger is first, so that you can win some real money—over $500 (Australian) is up for grabs. Your roach can then join former top-athlete roach winners in the Hall of Fame; former winners include Soft Cocky, Cocky Balboa, Cocky Dundee, Drain Lover, and Priscilla—Queen of the Drains.

If you can't psych-up your lowly friend for the main racing events, you won't necessarily be out of the money. You can build an elaborate cage for it, which you can then enter into the "Stable" contest, for the roach with the best crib.

Corbis/Richard T. Nowitz

Over 6,000 revelers from Australia, New Zealand, and the rest of the planet are on hand each year for this truly unique part of Australia Day. If your threshold for roaches is low, you can make do with other events. Prepare yourself for a big street party, with live music and other performances. This provides the perfect atmosphere in which to get to know a few native Aussies and try to figure out why they love cockroaches so much.

When You Go:

Stay at the site of the Cockroach Races, the Story Bridge Hotel, at 200 Main Street in Kangaroo Point. It's easy to spot because it's right next to the huge Story Bridge. The hotel was built in 1886 and renovated in the 1970s by its fun-loving owners, Richard and Jane Deery. In the evening, there is live entertainment with local bands at The Bombshelter, directly behind the hotel (it's an actual bomb shelter from World War II).

Web Coordinate:

www.whatsgoingon.com/100things/cockroach

> "the greatest
> gathering of
> thoroughbred
> cockroaches in
> the known
> universe"

Nyepi

Denpasar, Bali, Indonesia

GPS Lat: 08.65000 S Lon: 115.21666 E

Visitors to Bali usually expect to find Heaven on Earth but are often shocked upon arriving in the capitol, Denpasar, to find noisy traffic jams and beaches packed with loud beer-drinking Aussies. Granted, the interior of Bali is paradise. But there is one day each year, the Balinese *Saka* New Year, when the entire

Annual, March/April

island honors an observation of silence that permeates and transforms Bali into a surreal tropical daydream, completely devoid of noise and commotion.

This is Nyepi Day, a day of spiritual purification and retreat, of meditation and self-control, and a day free of bad spirits. Nyepi Day almost always takes place in March, on the first day of the tenth month of the Balinese lunar *Saka* calendar. The Balinese Hindu religion states that the new year should begin with nothingness, as all of existence came from nothing.

Nyepi is part of a series of four events over five days. The first is Melasti, three days before Nyepi, to purify the temple deities before the new year. This day is very colorful; people wear bright clothes and join hundreds of other celebrants in holy processions. Statues from the temples, where the deities live, are carried to the sea or to holy springs. Everyone prays, and the priest sprinkles holy water on the people to purify them in anticipation of Nyepi.

Next is Pengrupuk or Tawur Kesanga, the loud day before Nyepi, when evil spirits are driven away. Beginning at dusk, people bang pots and pans and carry torches through their houses. Then *ogoh-ogoh* demon effigies, made of wood, styrofoam, and bamboo, are carried through the streets in torch-lit parades.

On the morning of Nyepi, the spirits find the streets empty and purified from the prior day's activities, so they leave Bali alone. So as

> "an observation of silence that permeates and transforms"

not to break this good omen for the new year, everyone in Bali follows four Nyepi traditions: no light (including fire and cooking); no physical work; no entertainment (including music, art, and beauty); no leaving the home (most people don't even open their doors and windows). It is quiet, quiet, quiet, all day; it is a time for reflecting and gathering spiritual strength for the new year.

The day after Nyepi is Ngembak Nyepi. People visit each other and ask forgiveness for past mistakes. They also go to the mountains, lakes, and beaches. Sounds a lot purer than the hangovers that often begin the new year in the western world!

When You Go:

Hotels remain open on Nyepi Day, but services are reduced and some facilities—like those on the beach—are closed. Expect to spend a quiet day in your hotel room or restaurant. You'll likely be asked to keep the "no lights and curtains drawn" practice of the rest of the island. Airport transportation is available on a limited basis, so plan ahead. The only place on Bali you'll see light on Nyepi Day is at the airport.

Web Coordinate:

www.whatsgoingon. com/100things/nyepi

Danielle Rockhold Teplica

215

Rip Curl World Heli-Challenge

Wanaka, New Zealand

GPS Lat: 44.71666 S Lon: 169.16666 E

What do you get when you take those zany Kiwis and give them skis, snowboards, and helicopters? Broken bones. The Rip Curl World Heli-Challenge in Wanaka, New Zealand, is proof. It's the premiere alpine sporting competition in the Southern Hemisphere, and when New Zealanders host a sports event, you can be sure it will be extreme.

Annual, July/August

Around 200 of the world's top snowboarders and skiers and 10,000 spectators attend this helicopter-accessed powder skiing and boarding competition (you can't get there without a helicopter). Skiers and boarders compete in extreme, freestyle, and speed events.

Rip Curl Extreme Day is the hardest and most technical run of the week. For this event, snowboarders and skiers execute difficult runs down a daunting 2,000 vertical feet of mountain. Athletes dodge cliffs, rocks, and couloirs (deep gorges). They run over 80-foot airs (jumps), 300-foot thigh-burning arcs through deep powder, and, at times, steep 45-degree runs. The decisions they make often mean the difference between glory and a whole lot of hurtin'. The goal is to "flash it the most" during the run. Competitors are judged on control, form, technique, chosen line, and overall impression.

Rip Curl Freeride/Freeski Day is a bit less demanding (but not by much). Rip Curl is the only competition in the world that has an off-piste (off-trail), big-mountain freestyle run. Athletes must exhibit aerialist competence with flair, style, and fluidity on this natural terrain run. They face rollovers, undulating powder field terrain, rock outcroppings, and natural half pipes. It's rough stuff.

The best race to watch is the Rip Curl Chinese Downhill Day. In this speed event, all boarders and skiers charge off the top of the mountain at once, and the person who gets to the bottom first wins.

Tony Harrington at The Photo Shop, Wanaka

There are "no rules, just helmets" in this, the world's only "off-piste, hauling-arse, powder-burns" competition. Spectators are guaranteed to see lots of crashing, rolling, and fun injuries. Skiers have gone as fast as 62 mph in the Chinese Downhill Day event!

During the week, downtown Wanaka holds the legendary Streetstyle Big Air event. Snowboarders show their stuff on a ramp, Big Air gap jump, and 5-meter quarter-pipe, and invited demonstration teams show off for the crowd to the sounds of local bands. There's no better way to party with the pros!

When You Go:

Cardrona Ski Resort, located between Queenstown and Wanaka, offers free transportation to and from the airport in Queensland. Kiwis are outgoing, outdoorsy types, so there's not a whole lot going on indoors. Get in the spirit of sports and try bungee jumping or zorbing (a new extreme sport where people get in a giant plastic ball and are rolled down a hill), or taking skiing lessons. Be prepared for all kinds of weather—it changes quickly, sometimes without warning.

> "the premiere alpine sporting competition in the Southern Hemisphere"

Web Coordinate:

www.whatsgoingon.com/100things/ripcurl

Great Singsing at Mt. Hagen

Mt. Hagen Airport, Mt. Hagen, Papau New Guinea

GPS Lat: 05.52000 S Lon: 144.16000 E

Do you desire to see bearded men in loin-covers made of bark and women in grass skirts—all covered with motor oil? This dream will come true at Papau New Guinea's Great Singsing at Mt. Hagen. With its positive vibes and righteous intentions, this is a spectacular gathering spotlighting indigenous

Annual, August

Niuginian rituals of some very diverse tribes and clans.

In celebration of Papua New Guinea's culture, traditional tribal "colors" are sported . . . and then some. The theme of "people as art" brings travelers from all over the world for two days of the most outrageous costumes, facial painting, and exotic activity you are ever likely to experience.

The friendly competition takes place at the Mt. Hagen Airport and features an ocean of swirling feathers, bopping drums, and gyrating dancers. Hagen warriors, Huli wigmen, Chimbu mudmen and mudwomen, skeleton men, and a traditionally adorned Baisu women's group are but a few of the roughly fifty indigenous groups who strut their stuff.

Participants display fur necklaces, painstakingly arranged headdresses, shell wigs with specially cultivated flowers, and necklaces of hornbill beaks, feathers, and charcoal. Another interesting aspect of the gathering is the various paints and greases that the performers apply from their heads to their toes. Most of the paints come from minerals and plants, and the body grease is a combination of pig fat with ash and colorings. Motor oil is also favored by some, and car engines are often drained—sometimes to the surprise of the owners.

Essentially, the goal is for performers to outdo one another via eccentric costumes, body ornamentation, and wild dances. Stomping, chanting, pounding drum beats, swaying headdresses, and the music

Papau New Guinea Tourism Authority

of bamboo flutes, water pipes, and even electric guitars hooked up to portable radios make for quite the night out on the town. Judges score performers on a scale from 1 to 3, and winners are awarded a percentage of the event's admission charge.

The origin of the Singsing dates back to the 1950s, when the first Europeans who settled in the area thought a friendly assembly might be a good way to get the various clans to come together with the new settlers. Boy were they right!

When You Go:

Along with the Singsing competitions come nighttime dance parties, ceremonies, and feasts. Plan to spend several days. While you're there, don't forget that Papau New Guinea also offers some of the most fantastic scuba diving you can imagine, along with unparalleled natural beauty and wildlife. Consider a bushwalking trip, as August offers dry and (relatively) cool weather in the Highlands. A high risk of malaria exists all year in Papau New Guinea, so score some mefloquine before you go.

> "a spectacular gathering spotlighting indigenous Niuginian rituals"

Web Coordinate:

www.whatsgoingon.com/100things/singsing

Land Diving (Naghol)

Pentecost Island, Vanuatu

GPS Lat: 15.75000 S Lon: 168.16666 E

Annual, April/May
(Saturdays)

The remote island of Pentecost is home to the most thrilling fertility rite on earth—and the earliest form of bungee jumping. Centuries of expertise have cultivated "land diving," or *naghol*, daring jumps thought to fertilize the season's newly planted yams. Visitors have to pay big money to get a look at this ancient rite, but no outsiders are allowed to dive.

Land dives have been made by the men of Pentecost for over 1,500 years. Up to fifty divers jump on Saturdays in April and May. Vines tied around each ankle are cut to an exact length based on the diver's height so that the diver's head grazes the ground beneath and "fertilizes" it. Since the vines are stiff, not springy, divers are violently jerked back upward. If a vine is made a few centimeters too long, the diver could crush his skull. If it's a bit too short, he may break a few bones when he swings up against the diving tower. Still, there has only ever been one reported death.

Most local men of the remote island of Pentecost dive at least once in their lives. Young boys may dive once they are circumcised (around age eight). The diving tower can reach 85 feet in height, and the height of each diver's jump is determined by his age and experience. The jumper tells his most private feelings to the audience (often berating his wife) and then dives head first off the platform. The soil underneath is dug up to soften the blow of contact. The last and most exciting jump is done by the "Chief of the Tower" at the very top of the tower. Between jumps, women perform traditional chants and dances.

Land diving mythically stems from the fate of an abusive southern Pentecost tribesman, *Tamalié*. He chased his frightened wife high up into a tree, and she agreed to get back down with him only if he

220

would dive off the tree with her. He didn't know that she had tied two vines to her feet—she survived, and he plunged to his death. Women from the village started diving from trees, but tribal leaders decided that this was making the spirit of Tamalié angry and decreed that only men could make the jumps. Typical!

> "the most thrilling fertility rite on earth—and the earliest form of bungee jumping"

When You Go:

Vanuatu is about 500 miles northwest of Fiji, and isolation makes travel there expensive. Port Vila is the most accessible island and your best bet for accommodations. Then take a day-trip to see the land dives, which are expensive to attend (more than $350 per visitor and up to $1,000 if you take a video camera). Most inter-island travel is by airplane, offering a fabulous view of the islands. This time of year is winter in the southern hemisphere, which means 73-degree weather. Take lots of water to the dive.

Web Coordinate:

www.whatsgoingon.com/100things/landdiving

Carl Roessler

Indexes

About the Authors

About WhatsGoingOn.com

Acknowledgments

Index: Month by Month

*   Odd-numbered years
**   Every twelve years (2001, 2013, 2025)

Index: By Event and Location

Index: By Icon

Can See it on TV

Academy Awards Ceremony
Art Car Weekend
Bastille Day
Formula One Grand Prix of Monaco
Greenwich Village Halloween Parade
Mardi Gras
National Finals Rodeo
New Year's Eve in Times Square
Nobel Prize Ceremonies
Queen's Day (Koninginnedag)
Royal Ascot Races
Sydney Gay and Lesbian Mardi Gras

Celebrity Potential

Academy Awards Ceremony
Argentine Polo Finals (Campeonato Argentino Abierto)
Calgary Stampede and Exhibition
Cannes Film Festival
Carnaval
Chelsea Flower Show
Fez Festival of World Sacred Music
Formula One Grand Prix of Monaco
Love Parade
Mardi Gras
New Orleans Jazz and Heritage Festival
New Year's Eve in Times Square
Nobel Prize Ceremonies
Queen's Day (Koninginnedag)
Royal Ascot Races
Sydney Gay and Lesbian Mardi Gras
Vienna Opera Ball

Anastenaria Firewalking Ceremony
Ati-Atihan
Basque Herri Kilorak (Rural Sports)
Bastille Day
Battle of Gettysburg Reenactment
Bisket Jaatra
Calgary Stampede and Exhibition
Custer's Last Stand Reenactment
Darwin Beer Can Regatta
Great Singsing at Mt. Hagen
Hogmanay
Homowo (Hunger Hooting)
Iditarod Sled Dog Race
Il Palio di Siena
Incwala (Festival of the First Fruits)
International Dragon Boat Championships
Junkanoo
Kirkpinar Oil Wrestling Tournament
La Fiesta de la Virgen de la Candelaria
Land Diving (Naghol)
Las Fallas de Valencia
Los Diablos Danzantes (Devil Dancers of Corpus Christi)
Mardi Gras
Naadam
National Finals Rodeo
Navajo Nation Fair
Nobel Prize Ceremonies
Nyepi
Oktoberfest
Queen's Day (Koninginnedag)
Rath Yatra (Car Festival)
Running of the Bulls
Sanja Matsuri
Shuni-e (Omizutori)
Sydney Gay and Lesbian Mardi Gras
Tet Nguyen Dan
Up-Helly-Aa
World Championship Cockroach Races
World Cow Chip Throwing Championship

Dangerous

Anastenaria Firewalking Ceremony
Basque Herri Kilorak (Rural Sports)
Cannabis Cup
Cooper's Hill Cheese Roll
Dakar Rally
Formula One Grand Prix of Monaco
Icarus Cup Masquerade Flights (Coupe Icare)
Iditarod Sled Dog Race
Il Palio di Siena
Land Diving (Naghol)
Mangum Rattlesnake Derby
Marathon des Sables (Marathon of the Sands)
Naadam
National Finals Rodeo
Ngan Kin Jeh (Chinese Vegetarian Festival)
Rip Curl World Heli-Challenge
Running of the Bulls
Saut d'Eau Vodou Pilgrimage
Tough Guy
World Extreme Skiing Championships

Down and Dirty

Anastenaria Firewalking Ceremony
Ati-Atihan
Basque Herri Kilorak (Rural Sports)
Battle of Gettysburg Reenactment
Burning Man Project
Calgary Stampede and Exhibition
Cannabis Cup
Carnaval
Coaster Con
Cooper's Hill Cheese Roll
Custer's Last Stand Reenactment
Dakar Rally
Darwin Beer Can Regatta
Ganesh Chaturthi
Great Migration
Hogmanay
Holi

Hounen Matsuri (Tagata Fertility Festival)
Il Palio di Siena
International Dragon Boat Championships
Kirkpinar Oil Wrestling Tournament
La Tomatina
Land Diving (Naghol)
Los Diablos Danzantes (Devil Dancers of Corpus Christi)
Love Parade
Maha Kumbh Mela
Mangum Rattlesnake Derby
Marathon des Sables (Marathon of the Sands)
Mardi Gras
Naadam
National Finals Rodeo
Navajo Nation Fair
Oktoberfest
Pushkar Camel Fair
Roswell UFO Encounter
Running of the Bulls
Sanja Matsuri
Saut d'Eau Vodou Pilgrimage
Semana Santa
SPAMARAMA
Sydney Fringe Festival Nude Night Surfing
Testicle Festival
Tough Guy
Up-Helly-Aa
World Bog Snorkeling Championships
World Championship Punkin' Chunkin'
World Cow Chip Throwing Championship
World Extreme Skiing Championships

Ear Candy

Battle of Gettysburg Reenactment
Carnaval
Día de Los Muertos (Day of the Dead)
Fez Festival of World Sacred Music
Hogmanay
Hounen Matsuri (Tagata Fertility Festival)

Incwala (Festival of the First Fruits)
Great Singsing at Mt. Hagen
Junkanoo
La Fiesta de la Virgen de la Candelaria
Los Diablos Danzantes (Devil Dancers of Corpus Christi)
Love Parade
Mardi Gras
Mevlana Festival (Whirling Dervishes)
National Hollerin' Contest
New Orleans Jazz and Heritage Festival
Nyepi
Queen's Day (Koninginnedag)
Reveillon Rio
Sanja Matsuri
SPAMARAMA
Vienna Opera Ball

Family Affair

Art Car Weekend
Bastille Day
Battle of Gettysburg Reenactment
Calgary Stampede and Exhibition
Chung Yuan Ghost Month Festival
Custer's Last Stand Reenactment
Día de Los Muertos (Day of the Dead)
Hogmanay
Holi
Homowo (Hunger Hooting)
Icarus Cup Masquerade Flights (Coupe Icare)
Il Palio di Siena
International Dragon Boat Championships
Junkanoo
La Fiesta de la Virgen de la Candelaria
La Tomatina
Mangum Rattlesnake Derby
Monarch Butterfly Migration
Naadam
National Finals Rodeo
National Hollerin' Contest

North American Rainbow Gathering
Paris Air Show
Queen's Day (Koninginnedag)
Running of the Bulls
Sanja Matsuri
Sapporo Snow Festival
SPAMARAMA
Sydney Gay and Lesbian Mardi Gras
Venice Carnevale
World Championship Punkin' Chunkin'
World Cow Chip Throwing Championship

Gay and Lesbian Interest

Carnaval
Greenwich Village Halloween Parade
Love Parade
Mardi Gras
North American Rainbow Gathering
Queen's Day (Koninginnedag)
Sydney Gay and Lesbian Mardi Gras

Gluttony

Academy Awards Ceremony
Ati-Atihan
Calgary Stampede and Exhibition
Cannabis Cup
Carnaval
Chung Yuan Ghost Month Festival
Cooper's Hill Cheese Roll
Darwin Beer Can Regatta
Greenwich Village Halloween Parade
Hogmanay
Homowo (Hunger Hooting)
Hounen Matsuri (Tagata Fertility Festival)
Il Palio di Siena
Las Fallas de Valencia
Love Parade
Mangum Rattlesnake Derby
Mardi Gras
Navajo Nation Fair

New Orleans Jazz and Heritage Festival
New Year's Eve in Times Square
Oktoberfest
Queen's Day (Koninginnedag)
Reveillon Rio
Royal Ascot Races
Running of the Bulls
Sanja Matsuri
Semana Santa
SPAMARAMA
Sydney Gay and Lesbian Mardi Gras
Testicle Festival
Tet Nguyen Dan
Venice Carnevale

Grandma Approved

Chung Yuan Ghost Month Festival
Día de Los Muertos (Day of the Dead)
Fatima Pilgrimage
Monarch Butterfly Migration
National Hollerin' Contest
Pageant of the Masters
Roswell UFO Encounter
Royal Ascot Races
Sanja Matsuri
Sapporo Snow Festival
Semana Santa
Shuni-e (Omizutori)
Vienna Opera Ball
Yom Kippur at the Western Wall

Gross Things

Anastenaria Firewalking Ceremony
Coaster Con
Darwin Beer Can Regatta
Día de Los Muertos (Day of the Dead)
Hounen Matsuri (Tagata Fertility Festival)
La Tomatina
Mangum Rattlesnake Derby

Ngan Kin Jeh (Chinese Vegetarian Festival)
Saut d'Eau Vodou Pilgrimage
SPAMARAMA
Testicle Festival
World Bog Snorkeling Championships
World Championship Cockroach Races
World Cow Chip Throwing Championship

Jock Appeal

Argentine Polo Finals (Campeonato Argentino Abierto)
Basque Herri Kilorak (Rural Sports)
Calgary Stampede and Exhibition
Cooper's Hill Cheese Roll
Dakar Rally
Darwin Beer Can Regatta
Formula One Grand Prix of Monaco
Icarus Cup Masquerade Flights (Coupe Icare)
Iditarod Sled Dog Race
International Dragon Boat Championships
Kirkpinar Oil Wrestling Tournament
Land Diving (Naghol)
Marathon des Sables (Marathon of the Sands)
Naadam
National Finals Rodeo
Rip Curl World Heli-Challenge
Running of the Bulls
Sydney Fringe Festival Nude Night Surfing
Tough Guy
World Bog Snorkeling Championships
World Cow Chip Throwing Championship
World Extreme Skiing Championships

Loud as Hell

Anastenaria Firewalking Ceremony
Art Car Weekend
Ati-Atihan
Bastille Day
Battle of Gettysburg Reenactment
Bisket Jaatra

Burning Man Project
Calgary Stampede and Exhibition
Carnaval
Chung Yuan Ghost Month Festival
Coaster Con
Cooper's Hill Cheese Roll
Dakar Rally
Darwin Beer Can Regatta
Fez Festival of World Sacred Music
Formula One Grand Prix of Monaco
Ganesh Chaturthi
Great Migration
Great Singsing at Mt. Hagen
Greenwich Village Halloween Parade
Hogmanay
Holi
Homowo (Hunger Hooting)
Il Palio di Siena
International Dragon Boat Championships
Junkanoo
La Fiesta de la Virgen de la Candelaria
Las Fallas de Valencia
Love Parade
Maha Kumbh Mela
Mardi Gras
National Finals Rodeo
National Hollerin' Contest
New Orleans Jazz and Heritage Festival
New Year's Eve in Times Square
Ngan Kin Jeh (Chinese Vegetarian Festival)
Oktoberfest
Paris Air Show
Pushkar Camel Fair
Queen's Day (Koninginnedag)
Rath Yatra (Car Festival)
Reveillon Rio
Royal Ascot Races
Running of the Bulls
Sanja Matsuri

Saut d'Eau Vodou Pilgrimage
Shuni-e (Omizutori)
Sydney Fringe Festival Nude Night Surfing
Sydney Gay and Lesbian Mardi Gras
Tet Nguyen Dan
Up-Helly-Aa
Venice Carnevale
World Championship Cockroach Races
World Championship Punkin' Chunkin'

Mother Nature

Argentine Polo Finals (Campeonato Argentino Abierto)
Burning Man Project
Cannabis Cup
Chelsea Flower Show
Dakar Rally
Great Migration
Homowo (Hunger Hooting)
Icarus Cup Masquerade Flights (Coupe Icare)
Iditarod Sled Dog Race
Illumination of the Temple of Abu Simbel
Incwala (Festival of the First Fruits)
La Tomatina
Land Diving (Naghol)
Marathon des Sables (Marathon of the Sands)
Monarch Butterfly Migration
Namaqualand Wildflower Bloom
Navajo Nation Fair
North American Rainbow Gathering
Pushkar Camel Fair
Reveillon Rio
Rip Curl World Heli-Challenge
Sapporo Snow Festival
Sydney Fringe Festival Nude Night Surfing
Vernal Equinox at Chichen Itza

Academy Awards Ceremony
Art Car Weekend
Burning Man Project
Cannabis Cup
Coaster Con
Darwin Beer Can Regatta
Día de Los Muertos (Day of the Dead)
Great Migration
Hajj and Eid-al-Adha
Holi
Illumination of the Temple of Abu Simbel
Kirkpinar Oil Wrestling Tournament
La Tomatina
Land Diving (Naghol)
Las Fallas de Valencia
Los Diablos Danzantes (Devil Dancers of Corpus Christi)
Maha Kumbh Mela
Marathon des Sables (Marathon of the Sands)
Mevlana Festival (Whirling Dervishes)
Monarch Butterfly Migration
National Hollerin' Contest
Ngan Kin Jeh (Chinese Vegetarian Festival)
Nobel Prize Ceremonies
Nyepi
Pageant of the Masters
Paro Tsechu
Pushkar Camel Fair
Rath Yatra (Car Festival)
Santa Marta de Ribarteme "Near Death" Pilgrimage
Sapporo Snow Festival
SPAMARAMA
Testicle Festival
Tough Guy
Up-Helly-Aa
Venice Biennale
World Bog Snorkeling Championships
World Championship Cockroach Races
World Championship Punkin' Chunkin'
World Cow Chip Throwing Championship

Anastenaria Firewalking Ceremony
Ati-Atihan
Burning Man Project
Cooper's Hill Cheese Roll
Custer's Last Stand Reenactment
Dakar Rally
Fatima Pilgrimage
Great Migration
Great Singsing at Mt. Hagen
Hajj and Eid-al-Adha
Hounen Matsuri (Tagata Fertility Festival)
Icarus Cup Masquerade Flights (Coupe Icare)
Iditarod Sled Dog Race
Illumination of the Temple of Abu Simbel
Incwala (Festival of the First Fruits)
La Fiesta de la Virgen de la Candelaria
Land Diving (Naghol)
Los Diablos Danzantes (Devil Dancers of Corpus Christi)
Mangum Rattlesnake Derby
Marathon des Sables (Marathon of the Sands)
Monarch Butterfly Migration
Namaqualand Wildflower Bloom
National Hollerin' Contest
Navajo Nation Fair
North American Rainbow Gathering
Paro Tsechu
Pushkar Camel Fair
Rip Curl World Heli-Challenge
Santa Marta de Ribarteme "Near Death" Pilgrimage
Saut d'Eau Vodou Pilgrimage
Semana Santa
Testicle Festival
Tough Guy
Up-Helly-Aa
World Bog Snorkeling Championships
World Championship Punkin' Chunkin'
World Cow Chip Throwing Championship
World Extreme Skiing Championships

Potential to See Blood

Argentine Polo Finals (Campeonato Argentino Abierto)
Basque Herri Kilorak (Rural Sports)
Battle of Gettysburg Reenactment
Cooper's Hill Cheese Roll
Custer's Last Stand Reenactment
Dakar Rally
Formula One Grand Prix of Monaco
Iditarod Sled Dog Race
Il Palio di Siena
Kirkpinar Oil Wrestling Tournament
Mangum Rattlesnake Derby
Marathon des Sables (Marathon of the Sands)
National Finals Rodeo
Ngan Kin Jeh (Chinese Vegetarian Festival)
Rip Curl World Heli-Challenge
Running of the Bulls
Saut d'Eau Vodou Pilgrimage
Tough Guy
World Extreme Skiing Championships

Reenactments

Battle of Gettysburg Reenactment
Custer's Last Stand Reenactment
International Dragon Boat Championships
La Fiesta de la Virgen de la Candelaria
Pageant of the Masters
Roswell UFO Encounter
Santa Marta de Ribarteme "Near Death" Pilgrimage

Religious Fervor

Anastenaria Firewalking Ceremony
Ati-Atihan
Bisket Jaatra
Chung Yuan Ghost Month Festival
Día de Los Muertos (Day of the Dead)
Fatima Pilgrimage
Fez Festival of World Sacred Music
Ganesh Chaturthi

Hajj and Eid-al-Adha
Holi
Homowo (Hunger Hooting)
Hounen Matsuri (Tagata Fertility Festival)
Illumination of the Temple of Abu Simbel
Incwala (Festival of the First Fruits)
La Fiesta de la Virgen de la Candelaria
Land Diving (Naghol)
Las Fallas de Valencia
Los Diablos Danzantes (Devil Dancers of Corpus Christi)
Maha Kumbh Mela
Mevlana Festival (Whirling Dervishes)
Navajo Nation Fair
Ngan Kin Jeh (Chinese Vegetarian Festival)
Nyepi
Paro Tsechu
Pushkar Camel Fair
Rath Yatra (Car Festival)
Reveillon Rio
Sanja Matsuri
Santa Marta de Ribarteme "Near Death" Pilgrimage
Saut d'Eau Vodou Pilgrimage
Semana Santa
Shuni-e (Omizutori)
Tet Nguyen Dan
Vernal Equinox at Chichen Itza
Yom Kippur at the Western Wall

Shoppertunity

Battle of Gettysburg Reenactment
Chelsea Flower Show
Custer's Last Stand Reenactment
Día de Los Muertos (Day of the Dead)
Icarus Cup Masquerade Flights (Coupe Icare)
La Fiesta de la Virgen de la Candelaria
Mangum Rattlesnake Derby
Navajo Nation Fair
New Orleans Jazz and Heritage Festival
Pageant of the Masters

Paris Air Show
Pushkar Camel Fair
Queen's Day (Koninginnedag)
Roswell UFO Encounter
Sapporo Snow Festival

Snob Appeal

Academy Awards Ceremony
Argentine Polo Finals (Campeonato Argentino Abierto)
Cannes Film Festival
Chelsea Flower Show
Formula One Grand Prix of Monaco
Hogmanay
New Orleans Jazz and Heritage Festival
Nobel Prize Ceremonies
Pageant of the Masters
Paris Air Show
Queen's Day (Koninginnedag)
Royal Ascot Races
Venice Biennale
Venice Carnevale
Vienna Opera Ball

About the Authors

Dave Freeman and Neil Teplica decided to write *100 Things to Do Before You Die* shortly after founding WhatsGoingOn.com. They wanted to expose more of the amazing things they were discovering for their website. Both of them revel in the eccentricities of indigenous cultures and are fascinated at how festivals and events focus the local spirit.

Dave and Neil believe that travel can be life-changing, whether you're slumming it or being pampered. They believe that adventure and discovery across the zero- to five-star spectrum are more important than amenities. A great traveler can move seamlessly from New York to Nepal, from castles to campgrounds, and from fois gras to fried insects.

Friends for ages, Dave and Neil have traveled separately and together. Combined, they've covered over 2 million miles for pleasure and business. Dave has been known to stuff a tuxedo into a backpack, and Neil climbed Mt. Kilimanjaro on the way to an investment conference. Their bodies have surged with vaccinations and single-celled parasites in dozens of countries on five continents, and it seems there is never enough room in their passports.

About WhatsGoingOn.com

WhatsGoingOn.com is a new media travel company, serving as both fuel for your dreams and an aid in arranging your travel. Our focus is on the most active and sensory aspects of travel. We help you enjoy discovering yourself and new places, either on the road or from your living room. Hopefully, we'll help lead you over a great pass into adventure and exploration.

WhatsGoingOn.com is written by real people. In contrast to all the cookie-cutter travel resources out there, WhatsGoingOn.com endeavors to find the personality of places and to tell you what's going on in a clear and entertaining way. We do this by listening to people like you, and we always make room for your travel tips and experiences.

WhatsGoingOn.com and its Coolest Place on Earth® Today feature are internationally acclaimed and have been featured on TV and radio and in magazines and newspapers on all continents. As you read about your favorite events, we hope that you, too, will find WhatsGoingOn.com to be fun, informative, and helpful.

Acknowledgments

Special thanks to Yelena Gitlin.

Thanks to WhatsGoingOn.com's editors, past and present: Jennifer Coonce, James Dooley, Yelena Gitlin, Danielle Kiesler, Jack Lefelt, Laura Mendelsohn, Karen Polsky, Georgia Scurletis, Blair Woodward. You have all had a tremendous impact on this book.

Thanks to Nasser Al-Mansour for your knowledge about Hajj; Wes Alwan for being a superb editor of stories; David Arnsberger for cooking up the SPAMARAMA and for being such fun to talk to; José Ernesto Bravo from Lost World Adventures for tracking down a Diablos Danzantes photo; Andrew Bruck for your list; Mitch Caves from bootan.com for the basics on Paro Tsechu; Elan Cole for designing our icons; Vered Cole for your insights about Yom Kippur; Adrian Columb for digging deep in Australia; Shirley Crum a.k.a. Calamity Jane for your insights on Custer's Last Stand and Montana; the *Daily Journal* in Caracas for helping out on Diablos Danzantes information; John Dunlea for explaining the intricacies of cockroach racing; David Epstein for your knowledge of South Africa; David Escalante at ACE for explaining how ERT works; Andrew Farrell for baring all about nude surfing; Pascale Faubert for your Saut d'Eau and vodou insights; Jose Fernandez at the Spanish Government Tourist Office for dealing with our seemingly endless requests; Marion Fourerdier at the French Government Tourist Office for all your input; Mary Gadams for all your help with Marathon des Sables; Gordon Green for your background on bog snorkeling; Jason Haug for your Monty Python expertise; Thomas Hemba for the scoop on travel to Abu Simbel; Mark Johnson from WESC for your insights on extreme skiing; Rod "The Baron of Balls" Johnson for creating the Testicle Festival and for your recipe; Steve Hagar from *High Times* for the dope on Cannabis Cup; Roxanna Khan and Shauket Khan for your valuable insights on the festivals of India; Jason Kurisu at the Japan National Tourist Office for always being so helpful; Todd Lefelt for your book cover designs; Sophine Lim for your impressions of Venice Carnevale; George

McBean for setting us straight on the Serengeti Wildebeest Migration and for photo help; Patrick O'Hara for your observations about Reveillon; Julia Riley O'Sullivan for making sense of Morocco; Deirdre O'Shea for giving us the travel scoop on Ghana; Tony Peasley for your nuggets of wisdom on the art of cheese rolling; Robin Prestige and Marion Beverage at the British Tourist Authority for tracking down obscure Brits; Peter Roberts, Hillary Roberts, and Megan Coonce for the lowdown on the Rainbow Gathering; Bob Savage from Punkin' Chunkin' for great info; Ivan Small for knowing everything about weird Japanese festivals and Queen's Day; Ulrika Sundberg for the information on the Nobel Prize ceremonies; Anne Forschler Tarrasch and Jürgen Tarrasch for the Love Parade stories; Danielle Rockhold Teplica for your editing, contacts, and support; Doug Veith for your critical eye and design insights; Lisa Weitzman for your contributions about Israel; Peter Wirth for your Palio pointers.

Additional thanks to Jonas Abney; Barbara Carr; the Climbing Austrians and Poem Phone; Howard Cohen; the Coonce family; Mike Emmerich; Dag Folger; Fred Francis; Roy Freeman; Virginia Freeman; Delia Guzman; Charles Hamilton, Katie Otey, and Alex Struminger at Planetrider.com; Risa Mickenberg; Hewitt Pratt; Robert Schmunk; Arlene Sepulveda; Stacey Sexton; Ken Stuart at Gilbert, Segall and Young LLP; Tastee D-Lite Hotline; Joseph Teplica; Lorene Torrey; Sarah Tollett; Jessica Wainwright at The Literary Group.